# Watch Your Words

*To all those from whom I have received a legacy
and who have made me what I am.*

# Watch Your Words

## A Manifesto for the Arts of Speech

GÉRALD GARUTTI

Translated and with a foreword by
Raymond Geuss

polity

Originally published in French as *Il faut voir comme on se parle: Manifeste pour les arts de la parole.* © Actes Sud, 2023

This English translation © Polity Press, 2025

Foreword © Raymond Geuss 2025

Polity Press
65 Bridge Street
Cambridge CB2 1UR, UK

Polity Press
111 River Street
Hoboken, NJ 07030, USA

ISBN-13: 978-1-5095-6729-4

A catalogue record for this book is available from the British Library.

Library of Congress Control Number: 2024943768

Typeset in 11 on 13 pt Sabon
by Cheshire Typesetting Ltd, Cuddington, Cheshire
Printed and bound in Great Britain by CPI Group (UK) Ltd, Croydon

The publisher has used its best endeavours to ensure that the URLs for external websites referred to in this book are correct and active at the time of going to press. However, the publisher has no responsibility for the websites and can make no guarantee that a site will remain live or that the content is or will remain appropriate.

Every effort has been made to trace all copyright holders, but if any have been overlooked the publisher will be pleased to include any necessary credits in any subsequent reprint or edition.

For further information on Polity, visit our website:
politybooks.com

# Contents

# Foreword

The best manifestos are punchy, pungent, and constructive. They are discursively elaborated and supported rallying
cries. They often have a clear tripartite structure: they diag-
nose some lack or deficiency or defect in our world, they then
articulate an aspiration for a better state of the world, and
finally they propose a course of action and attempt to motivate
readers to adopt it. 'Proletarians of the world, unite! You have
nothing to lose but your chains.' This is a good, brief summary
of the *Communist Manifesto*: what is wrong with nineteenth-
century industrial society is the very existence of a large group
of people who have no choice but to sell their labour as a
commodity in order to survive; the aspiration is for a society
without classes and the course of action proposed is for the
members of the proletariate to unite and act to abolish private
ownership of the means of production. The manifesto of the
Centre for the Arts of Speech which you are about to read
has an equally clear message that can also be summed up very
briefly: *speaking is acting, so cultivate the arts of speech.*

The simple, apparently trivial statement that to speak is to
act turns out, on inspection, to be more complicated than it
seems and also more consequential. Obviously, if I say to my

taxi driver, 'Stop the car here,' I am performing an action, and
one which intends to bring about a change in the world, but
equally if I say to someone, 'You half-wit,' I am doing something, namely insulting the person so addressed. Suppose that,
when he was Prime Minister, Boris Johnson had announced
that Brexit had increased the UK's GDP. If I then, the next
day, had published statistics that indicated a decline in GDP,
I would have contradicted him, whether or not I had intended
to do so. This does not mean that there is no difference between
intentionally contradicting someone and doing it unintention-
ally; these are different actions, but still both are acts. I can, of
course, abstract from the *immediate* action-context of what
someone says. It is perfectly possible to create practices (or
even institutions) that allow one to focus merely, for instance,
on the correctness of the statistics I have gathered, irrespective
of the political uses to which they can be put. One can argue
about how complete the hermetic isolation from immediate
action can ever be, but even if one were to grant for the sake of
argument that the Institute for Statistics was a kind of Platonic
Academy, the discussions there would not be non-actions, but
especially complex actions.

In principle, actions can always be evaluated ethically, morally, politically, and aesthetically. Was it right to tell the taxi
driver to stop? Was Boris Johnson's speech elegantly phrased
and presented? Was it effective? Was it prudent? Was this a
good time for me to draw attention to the failures of Brexit?
Some actions can also be evaluated alethetically, that is, some,
although not all of them, can purport to assert truths. If I
say that GDP is down 4.5 per cent, I can investigate to what
extent that statement is well confirmed, well supported, or
even (if I care to use that term) 'true'. Nothing exactly parallel holds for 'Stop the car here.' I may have made all kinds
of mistakes in issuing this command – I may think we are
approaching St Pancras Station, where I can get Eurostar,
but it is actually Euston Station – and the injunction may in

some sense be 'wrong', or 'misguided', but it is not exactly 'false'.

If speech is a kind of action, it, too, is in principle subject to all these multiple forms of evaluation. This is true with the usual proviso, namely that for particular purposes we may wish to act so as to suspend specific kinds of evaluations in certain contexts. The complexity of this kind of action – suspension of our evaluative attitudes – is one of the reasons it is so difficult for us to decide whether or not, for instance, we should, as Simone de Beauvoir proposed, 'burn de Sade'.[1]

The diagnostic portion of this manifesto begins by pointing to a series of disagreeable and destructive phenomena, many of which, individually, will be familiar, in one way or another, to people who live in a contemporary Western society. The loss of basic civility in public discourse and the consequent coarsening of public debate has often been noted and is much discussed. To take one particularly egregious example, think of the campaign speeches of Donald Trump, which often amount to little more than the repetition of strings of insulting nicknames for his political opponents and vulgar abuse. The absence of graciousness and common courtesy might seem to be a very minor vice, if it were not for the fact that experience shows us that this form of behaviour is always on the verge of spilling over into threats of and calls for direct violence. No public discussion was, perhaps, ever completely rational (whatever that means), but one has crossed an important frontier and entered a significantly darker world when a British minister can say that people 'have had enough of experts' and can glory in this fact. We are in danger of losing the very idea that political actors could be expected to give reasoned, empirically based arguments for the positions they adopt.

This degradation of public discourse seems to go hand in hand with the increasing isolation of individuals, with the intensification of feelings of impotence and lack of agency, with loss of a wider sense of purpose in our actions, and with an impoverishment of all those portions of the human soul, including our very sense of self, that require regular nourishment from sociability.

Part of the originality of Gérald Garutti's project is to propose a way of seeing all these developments as part of a single complex syndrome. He analyses what is happening as the breakdown of 'speech'. 'Speech', for Garutti, is a technical term which, however, also has direct empirical reference. On the one hand, 'speech' (and the terms semantically associated with it) can be used to refer to familiar everyday events such as conducting a conversation at the dinner table, addressing a group of people at a funeral or wedding, explaining to a dentist why you have booked an appointment, telling a joke, or reciting a poem for a group of children. In this sense, 'speech' looks like a normal empirical concept, but it has another side or another dimension for which there is no generally recognized designation. Above, I called it 'technical', but one might think of it as 'aspirational', 'exigent', 'ideal', or 'normative'. In this dimension, calling some forms of human verbal behaviour 'speech' is not simply noticing some actual properties which they exhibit, but evaluating them tacitly relative to some desiderata, or subjecting them, at least in imagination, to some demands. Speech refers to a large set of properties which human behaviour 'should' instantiate. Garutti mentions some of these desiderata: focusing on what other people are saying, listening to them carefully, expressing what one has to say clearly and honestly, waiting one's turn before speaking. This list is clearly not comprehensive and is not intended to be; in fact it is hard to see how it could be completely comprehensive because it is a characteristic of this domain of human life that it be open to development; the list is there to be added to. We can always imagine listening with greater care, just as we can always imagine that there will be new demands we will want to impose on human behaviour which we cannot concretely envisage now. The 'aspiration' articulated here – the second part of a classical manifesto – is that speech be allowed to come into its own and be itself.

A certain kind of philosopher would be likely at this point to say that what I have done is point out an 'ambiguity' in the term 'speech': it is sometimes used as an empirical concept and sometimes as a normative concept, and so its meaning shifts. This way of approaching the matter obscures an important point by suggesting that concepts like this are in some sense deficient, and should (and *could*) be replaced by a set of sharply contrasted and semantically more abstemious terms. What this misses is that the whole rationale of concepts like 'speech' (as Garutti uses it) is to claim an inherent connection between the two aspects: the empirical and the aspirational. A lot more could be said about the nature of this 'connection', and Garutti makes as good a beginning of doing this as one can expect within the narrow limitations of a brief 'manifesto'. His account is also refreshing and plausible, partly because he avoids a narrow focus on *one* (purportedly) essential link between the two conceptions and tries to acknowledge the multiplicity of historically specific, and morally and politically significant, connections.

The parallel is not exact, but for a vague analogy think of our use of terms like 'democracy/democratic'. Only a particularly narrow-minded pedant would object to someone saying, 'Ancient Greek democracy was not really very democratic (because it excluded women and slaves).' We call it a 'democracy' because it had some recognizable empirical properties – political decisions were made by voting in a mass assembly – but we deny that it was 'democratic' because these empirical properties of the system are valued *as* ways in which some ideal of 'the power of the people' (*demo-kratia*) or the self-governance of the *whole* population is realized, and we can see that this was not the case in fifth-century Athens. I note that the Greeks themselves were perfectly aware of discrepancies of this kind. Thucydides writes that during the period when

Pericles was most powerful in Athens the city was a 'democracy' in name only and actually it was ruled by the foremost man.[2] The structures of the democracy operated as usual, but they did not work as exercises of the power of the *people*. The population as a whole did not really make decisions; Pericles made them. (Thucydides gives this analysis his own particular twist in that he thinks it was actually *better* for the Athenians to have decisions made for them by Pericles than to have decided things themselves, but that is a further point that is not directly relevant here.) Equally we can perfectly well say, 'People in this society are *talking* to each other all the time, incessantly, without interruption, but there is very little *speech* taking place.'

It is cognitively disadvantageous, then, to make a fuss about an 'ambiguity' in the term 'speech' because the point of the construction is precisely to emphasize the connection between the two dimensions. Similarly, when I began this foreword by writing 'speaking is acting', one might (rightly) point out that this English sentence has no parallel in any single French sentence in Garutti's text. 'Speaking is acting' can be taken in one (or both) of two different ways. First, I act when I speak just as I act when I brush my teeth in the morning, or feed the cat, make a cup of tea, or close the front door. This is 'act' in the sense of *faire, agir, se comporter*, and so forth. However, to 'act' in English also has an important second use, and in this second sense 'to act' means to perform on the stage, take part in a theatrical production, or play a role. This is *jouer, représenter*. Again, though, the point is the connection, which turns out to be not too difficult to see, once one has begun to look in the right direction. Anything that can count as the performance of a properly human action is to some extent dependent on something that is very much like playing a role in a theatrical production. It is by mimicking others that one learns to do anything that goes beyond pulling one's hand out of a fire or searching out the mother's breast for milk. Thus the relevant centrality of the theatrical models that occur in the book. Those old eighteenth-century dichotomies so beloved of followers of Rousseau – natural/artificial, authentic/contrived, spontaneous/imitative, even sincere/insincere – have their place in human life, to be sure, but it is a distinctly subordinate, not a fundamental one. No version of these distinctions is absolute, catgeorically binding, or set in stone once and for all. Both Montaigne and Nietzsche saw this clearly, and drew the consequences.

To put it another way, truly human action is action informed by and dependent on speech in a variety of ways. Even Robinson Crusoe is not speech-less on his island; he reads his Bible (in English) and the first thing he does with Friday is teach him a language which he himself acquired from other speakers of English. Since language is a shared human practice, it can only be acquired through interaction with other humans who already speak, by a series of actions that are not completely spontaneous, but intentionally shaped in a particular way. Perhaps human beings have in themselves something that can reasonably be called a 'natural' impulse to produce sounds and a natural tendency to mimic and imitate, but these result in Mandarin, or French, or Xhosa 'speech' only when they regularly and reliably have a structure and form which has been imposed on them by humans in interaction. Herodotus in Book II of his *Histories* reports that King Psammeticus of Egypt had two infants raised without contact with any other humans, apart from one shepherd who came to feed them. He did this in order to find out what language they would speak, as it were spontaneously or naturally. Psammeticus was told that the noises they produced were a form of Phrygian, because one of the 'words' they pronounced had some vague similarity with a Phrygian word that would have been an appropriate thing to say in the context, but we would be more inclined, I think, to take them to be just a form of burbling (on the part of the children) plus wishful thinking (on the part of the adults).

Acquiring a language, even a first language, is, in other, words proto-theatre. I learn to speak by learning to adopt a role, or, actually, many roles, in reality and in the imagination, and only then am I capable of properly human action. Even the mastery of such a simple thing as the use of pronouns requires me to put myself in imagination in your, his, her, its, or their position; otherwise I would never be able to understand such simple exchanges as 'How are you?'/'I am fine, and you?' And if I eventually learn to depart from aspects of that role, or to write a new part for myself, or to improvise – which is acquiring a capacity that most thinkers in the modern world take to be an especially important one – this is because I have internalized a wide variety of forms and modes of speech, roles, and plots, and have learned to go beyond them. Garutti rightly condemns the tendency to reduce the public representation of human life to a series of eight highly clichéd stereotypes derived ultimately from debased theatrical sources, but this criticism is not some kind of purist insistance that drama or literature has – or ought to have – no place at all in the structuring of human interactions, but rather that these are overly simplified patterns of behaviour.

'Cliché', of course, is an aesthetic category, or rather an aesthetico-ethical one, because it is a formula that by simplifying our perception in a certain way makes it difficult for us to discern highly relevant complications and singularities. To operate with clichés is both aesthetically repellent (because the boredom induced by tired repetition of well-known formulae is the exact reverse of the surprise and excitement that good art engenders in its audience) and morally reprehensible (because perceptual obtuseness is an obstacle to good action). It is another one of the particular great strengths of Garutti's book that he does not treat 'aesthetics' (in the broadest sense) as something separate and distinct that must be kept at a distance, an add-on, a luxury, or an afterthought. The imaginative organization of our action according to tacit principles of euphony, rhythm, parallelism, and symmetry, increasing and decreasing tension and the resolution of that tension, pleasing ideational association, analogy, and so forth, is not an extra that one can take or leave *ad libitum*, nor is it something that can be left to special occasions, or relegated to special disciplines that chug along their own track without impinging on the serious concerns of living. Whether we know it or not, and whether we like it or not, 'aesthetic' structures are constitutents of the very fabric of human life at a very elemental level, and they thus are part of the way our social world really works.

In the final portion of his text, Garutti outlines some of the projects and initiatives which he has undertaken at CAP, the Centre for the Arts of Speech (Centre des arts de la parole) in Paris, and the immediate action-motivating aspect of his manifesto is to solicit support for enterprises like this one and to encourage people to cultivate the arts of speech in whatever other ways are possible. Some people might find this insufficiently radical politically. The deepest reason, they might claim, for speechlessness, lack of a sense of agency, and disorientation is societal coercion, real deprivation, poverty, oppression, and the only real remedy for that is fundamental socio-economic change of a kind that is beyond the scope of a project like the one outlined in this manifesto.

There are several reasons why this is not really a relevant objection. First, Garutti is not so naïve as to propose the cultivation of speech as a panacea for all social ills. In addition to his other many accomplishments, he is one of the world's great experts on Bertolt Brecht, so perhaps it is not completely inappropriate to suggest that in reading this book one thinks of Brecht's poem 'Die Nachlager'. This poem is about a man during the Great Depression of the 1930s in the US who solicited the *ad hoc* provision of free accommodation for the unemployed and homeless, one night at a time. The poem continues:

*Die Welt wird dadurch nicht anders*
*Die Beziehungen zwischen den Menschen verbessern sich nicht*
*Das Zeitalter der Ausbeutung wird dadurch nicht gekürzt*
*Aber einige Männer haben ein Nachlager*
*Der Wind wird von ihnen eine Nacht lang abgehalten*
*Der ihnen zugedachte Schnee fällt auf die Straße.*

[The world is not transformed by this/ Relations between people
are not improved/ The era of exploitation is not shortened/ But
a few men get a bed for the night/ The wind is kept off them for
one night/ Snow that was meant for them, falls on the street.]

Cultivating speech is like providing a bed for the night. It is not
the universal solution to all our problems – much less to all
human problems *simpliciter* – but it is also not nothing.

There is a second and deeper reason, which reveals something important about 'speech'. The possible criticism which
was just canvassed tacitly assumes that 'speech' is to be treated
in one or another of two ways, both of which, however, are
actually inappropriate. Either good speech is just something
like a commodity or consumer good (a bed for the night), or
the demand to improve the quality of speech in a society is
exclusively a therapeutic one, that is, the demand that one deal
with some palpable malfunction in social life. Good speech,
however, is not a commodity that can be bought, sold, traded,
exchanged for something else, because, correctly understood,
it is the kind of thing the value of which is in some sense
incommensurable. The second point is that the temptation
to fall back on medical, therapeutic, or hygienic models here
is almost irresistible, but we must resist it. Pressure toward
the medical model seems virtually built into the structure of
a manifesto, as I have described it, so I might seem myself to
have succumbed to this temptation at the beginning of this
foreword when I spoke about Garutti giving the diagnosis of
a 'syndrome'. This way of thinking is attractive partly because

it is not completely wrong – degraded speech *can* be seen as an organic dysfunction in a society – but it leaves out what is in many ways the most important thing. Speech is not just a domain in which defects and obstructions must be removed, so that 'normal', 'healthy' functioning can be assured; it is a realm that is inherently utopian, the place (which is also 'no-place') where we create ways of going beyond our immediate environment and our given selves. It is not merely that it has value 'in itself' (as some philosophers might say) and is not just a necessary prop for supporting social reproduction and good decision-making. Speech is what allows the human here-and-now to exist at all, because there is no here-and-now outside a relation to possible *other* places, different possible futures, to the past and to imagined alternative worlds – objects of aspiration, hope, terror, delight, contempt. The possibility of such worlds is what speech creates. In one of his early works, the philosopher Ludwig Wittgenstein wrote: 'The world of the happy man is different from that of the unhappy man.'[3] In *this* sense of 'world' (not the sense in which Brecht uses the term in his poem cited above), the 'world' in a society in which speech is cultivated is *not* the same as one in which it is not.

The poems of Sappho, Sulpicia, and Baudelaire, the novels of Woolf, Proust, Kafka, and Musil, the works of Aristophanes, Rabelais, Cixous, and Madame de Staël: these are not correctly construed as the contents of a kind of social apothecary. How *are* they to be correctly construed?

Ah, that is the question. Welcome to the world of speech!

Raymond Geuss

# Part I

# The diminution of our humanity

# The radical degradation of speech

# 1

# Watch how you speak

## Speech as a combat sport

### When speech dislocates the world

We live in a world of sound and fury; a world dominated by information technology, by the clicks and clacks of a keyboard. A world of rumours, of tweets, of bashing and clashing, of fake news, swipes, and wars of words: of *LOL* and *like*. It is a digital world of finger-pointing, governed by a new Index of Prohibited Words, Thoughts, and Authors (even though this Index is no longer drawn up by the Vatican) where a new form of thumbs-up (or thumbs-down) can decide one's fate and with a global pillory in which deviants can be locked and exhibited. The world is now a global network where a single word can kill.

Never before has humanity done so much talking. This situation is historically without precedent and in many respects it represents an almost unimaginable opportunity. Everyone is constantly expressing themselves, letting themselves go, explaining their views at great length, sounding off, taking offence, starting arguments. Constant chattering is everywhere. But is anyone listening? For that matter, are people even speaking *to* each other? What kind of game is being played here? Who is it who is speaking? Now everyone has a voice, can take a public position, or even shout it from the rooftops. In one sense, that gives everyone a chance to speak, but what kind of chance is that in reality? The answer depends very much on who is speaking, what they are saying, in whose name they claim to speak, whom they are addressing, on the 'how' and 'why' of their intervention.

Just look at how we speak and see how much our humanity has been diminished. How are we using this exceptional power – speech – which we possess? In the contemporary world, we are witnessing a catastrophic degradation of the realm of speech: enunciation becomes denunciation, stigmatization, destruction. Words divide, whether or not they are spoken with destructive intention. For many of us, they have lost their meaning. Speech nowadays is not a domain in which reflection takes place, but one in which linguistic tokens devoid of sense are deployed in a violent game, where the destructive turmoil on the surface actually has the effect of removing important things from our field of vision, and covering over what is essential. For us today, the realm of speech has overwhelmingly become a space of concealment and distortion.

We suffer from verbal inflation; our discourse is devalued; our messages become worthless; what we say is no longer creditworthy. The conditions under which exchanges take place have deteriorated, and the value of the Other has been massively reduced. This, at any rate, is the direction in which things are moving. The flood of words becomes a mere vehicle for the expression of momentary and unmediated impulses. Logorrhoea goes hand in hand with an increasing lack of content. All that is left is blind vanity, which leaves open a place that is occupied by increasingly radical, and increasingly irresponsible, assertions.

Even as it proliferates, speech, in many of its contemporary forms, is undergoing a process of degradation. The result is a trivialization and instrumentalization of one of our most precious resources. It becomes a means of dividing and humiliating people, and of making them cruder and coarser than they were. The destruction of meaning debases the speaker while degrading the listener. The social bond is torn apart.

*Speech is essential and must be properly valued and esteemed*

This text makes a simple appeal: we must value speech properly; otherwise the current explosion of forms of expression, far from being a sign that we are treating our common humanity as a sacred trust, will rather be an indicator of our social atomization. Who are we and by what right do we make such an appeal? We are artists of the spoken word, artisans of speech in action, workers engaged in the maintenance of the social bond; we tell stories and pass on history, we create meaning and open up spaces in which people can encounter each other directly. We speak in the name of arts that are already three thousand years old. Arts which since the dawn of time have shaped the human heart, and have laboured, over the course of ages, to allow our humanity to emerge and express itself. Arts which even today make us all a very generous offer: they offer us the possibility of transcending ourselves.

We think that the cultivation of speech is more vital today than ever because speech by its very nature is what brings our social existence to life. Understood in the fullest and most substantial sense, speech expresses our quintessence. It is an essential domain which is never irrelevant. This is because it is the place where meaning is crystallized, discourse intersects with action, and thought gets its motivational power. If it is properly thought through and inspired, and appropriately focused on its audience, speech manifests the power of verbal articulation and the resonance of words, and it brings texts to life in the present. When it is shared among the members of a real existing community, it gives each one a public presence,

allowing them to take a position and give an opinion; oral presentation is the life-blood of language, what gives it substance.
It is multifarious in its functions and uses, and precisely for
that reason it encompasses all the dimensions of our life.

## Against the impoverishment of speech

We refuse to reduce speech to any of its aetiolated spectres:
to mere disruptive shouting or sly insinuation; to the mere
conformist repetition of 'what people say' or gossip which pur-
ports to give the reader the inside dope; to mere chatter or to
just a spray of words that pulverize and humiliate. Speech that
is broken up into a mere succession of pitiful slogans, sound-
bites, laughable 'messages', and empty platitudes held together
by an empty shell of syntax is an eviscerated caricature of itself.

We refuse to allow language and speech to be remade in
the sad image of those Four Musketeers of the contemporary
world: Fake News, Clashos, Bashos, and Box Office.

We will not make way for those who wish to give the last
word to 'the image' on the grounds that it, we are told, 'tells
the whole story'. We who are speaking to you know that the
visible is not everything; that which is essential is invisible to
the human eye. In some sense, even the ear is an organ of
procreation because babies come from our using our ears and
listening.[1]

In the beginning was the word, but now in the end it is verbiage that is accumulating. We are not prepared to accept that
the globalization of speech must be a process of dilapidation,
and language a more and more standardized and homogene-
ous 'product'. The transformation of speech into a commodity
to be bought and sold on the mass market is a form of alienation and degradation. Meaning comes to be atomized, reduced
to disconnected elements that are themselves mere grains of
nothingness. Thought cannot be reduced to slogans, info-bites,
or clichés, as it is in the world of 'two tweets, three seconds,

four emoticons, two hundred and eighty characters'. We are not prepared to grant to the medium the unrestricted, sole power to determine all content, and to see in it nothing but a mere flux of constantly shifting impressions.

We reject the culture of the disposable word, fit only to be thrown on the rubbish heap immediately after use. We are people who exert ourselves to the utmost, working patiently day and night to find a way through the mass of empty claims floating on the surface of the Lethe: the River of Forgetfulness. Our goal is to arrive at a place where we can construct, through our work, what the Greek historian Thucydides called 'a possession which will last for all time'.[2] Chatter passes away; speech remains, and it is speech which holds us in thrall; which allows us to keep our feet on the ground and maintain our balance; which undergirds the very existence of a 'we'; which connects us with everything.

In a world of universal cacophony, we choose instead the resonance of that which is essential. We choose the passion of interaction over the tyranny implicit in the slogan 'it's all about me'. We prefer the gentle susurrus of language to the loud braying of opinion, the weight of meaning to the emptiness of formulae, the intensity of attention to the inanity of channel-surfing. We prefer to assume the responsibility of articulating a position rather than simply engaging in non-committal palaver. Rather than withdraw behind a computer screen, we choose the communion which is established when different people are physically in one another's presence. The virtual realm is a realm of impunity, but we prefer real embodied experience with all its vulnerability and responsibilities. Instead of the complacency of brute force, we choose conscientious application of skill in addressing one another: we welcome difference instead of being perpetually on the look out for 'deviancies' to reject. We prefer the culture of exchange to the cult of the self; shared humanity to the simulacra of 'community' which the media offer.

We ground our work, our action, our motivation – our very existence – on speech. We cannot but note the denigration and degeneration which speech has had to endure in the contemporary world. Knowing all the facts, we have taken the full measure of the destruction this dire state of affairs has wrought. This is precisely why we make it our aim here to begin the process of re-establishing the paramount value of speech in contemporary society. Discharging the task we have set ourselves will require us to question the role of speech in society, to elucidate its functions, to affirm its place, and to bear witness to its vocation.

## The deluge of jibes

Some might object that in pursuing this project we are swimming against the tide – or even acting contrary to good sense – that we are conducting a rear-guard action against an inevitable fate. We are shadow-boxing against wholly imaginary speaking monsters of our own creation. The words they speak exist only in minds that have been deranged by too much reading of printed books. In fact, as the pyromaniac fireman in Ray Bradbury's *Fahrenheit 451* says, just before burning a huge stack of books, it is complete lunacy to believe anything they contain, because they all contradict each other.[3] This in itself is an indication that in fact a tweet is incomparably better than its fossilized ancestor, the book, and is a thousand times more valuable. The tweet, after all, is more up-to-the-minute, more immediate, more concise, more spontaneous, more edgy, and more viral. Isn't that, after all, a guarantee that a form of speech is truly *authentic*? Look at Donald Trump: a post, one more post-truth – and let no one say 'what a lie', because that would be so passé.

Our critics will present us as a group of disgruntled, old-school literary types, obsessed with the past, and rendered irrelevant by the arrival of the new Gospel for the modern world which announces the advent of a digital absolutism. We are, they will claim, a band of smooth-talking oldies, who still rely on (and continue to advocate) archaic verbal canons, at a time when modern people are adventurously navigating the World Wide Web, full speed ahead, driven forward by the wind of modern technology. We are, they say, bitter-enders, left-over humanists, already swept into the dustbin of history with no place in the new age of electronically and genetically enhanced humans, and of a post-human world. We are nothing but a cabinet of historical curiosities. We stand there frozen and petrified at the very sight of our contemporary *re-post-modernity*, that age in which one simply re-transmits electronically things which no one needs to understand. The 're-post' is the ideal expression of the herd instinct and of lemming-like conformism, where responding is an automatic reaction, a matter of replying without reflecting. Where one does down without building up. This post-post-modern world is one of complete entropy. Our opponents will try to steamroller us, shouting that 'It is too late; the die has already been cast; E-story has now killed off – and has replaced – history. Capital 'E' is not just for 'Electronic', but also for 'Eviscerate', 'Eliminate', and 'Erase'. It is, they will say, necessary to make a *tabula rasa* for all those novel developments that are to come, and they are coming from all sides, more and more of them and at a constantly accelerating rate. Our opponents repeat *ad nauseam* their claim that speech has never been in a more flourishing state – just look around, isn't it obvious? Nowadays it rules in triumph everywhere, penetrates every domain without limits or constraints, without frontiers. Speech is infinitely polymorphous and unendingly prolific.

Our detractors will try to mobilize against us a purported opposition between, on the one hand, the sacred right of everyone to express themselves as they wish and, on the other, our elitist conceptions which allow us to usurp for ourselves the right to define what counts as 'good', 'correct', or 'beautiful' verbal usage. We are, they say, the last representatives of an archaic way of thinking and speaking, as it were, the last battalion left standing. Our 'aristocratic conception' of speech, however, will be swept away by the new 'democr@tic revolution', which will be a cultural Great Leap Forward, in which the World Wide Web will make it possible for everyone to talk all the time to anyone they please. There will be millions and millions of New Gospels *in secula seculorum. Halleluia!* We should be celebrating this new culture available to everyone online, accessible to anyone at any time. To be sure, does the word *'culture'* still have any meaning in this context – even if in the plural? In the new 'democr@cy, everyone is free to insist on their own form of expression, because, in principle, all forms of expression are now to count as equally good. It might even be taken to be grounds for self-congratulation that finally *expression* has succeeded in swallowing up and thus putting an end to *art*, that fundamentalist religion whose followers took themselves to be something special. Good riddance to *'art'*; that luxury which was for so long the reserved domain of a gang of over-privileged snobs, who dare to claim that although all art is expression, not all expression is art. The final touch of this delightful line of thought is to press back into service that old war-horse 'the elite and the people', and to brand us as the final avatars of the former. 'A small minority of the self-proclaimed *crème de la crème* against the masses of common folk': this tired old cliché of demagogues seems never to wear out, and is still effective. It gives our opponents some satisfaction to be able to trot out these stereotypes, adjust them slightly, and claim to discover an antagonism between 'the people' and 'artists', that unreformable caste of misfits living in their ivory towers, who are really just highly articulate dinosaurs left over from the pre-history of language, and who will now finally be drowned in the waves of the new irresistible deluge which represents the future. QED.

We need to pass beyond these false dichotomies which are

imposed on us by people engaged in constant recriminations against their imaginary opponents, despite the fact that our age seems to have an infinite appetite for them. They are at best reductive parodies. We know in advance that they will be deployed, but we must nevertheless put them aside. Still the legitimate question remains: what exactly are we talking about?

## Speech is a weapon of war

*The speech organ. Speech as the highest power*

What is at issue in this section is 'speech' in the sense in which we sometimes use that term, namely a form of human activity which is precisely not directed at attaining or expressing truth, much less justice, but which is a human power. 'It is speech, speech not action that rules the world': this is what Ulysses says at the beginning of Sophocles' *Philoctetes*.[4] This single, simple phrase expresses a whole conception of speech, its essence, and its function, and one that has become predominant. Ulysses was the epitome of the speaker in this sense. He is *'polytropos'*, to give him his Homeric epithet,[5] that is, he is the man of many wiles and dodges *par excellence*. He *always* has a number of further tricks up his sleeve, and he is so quintessentially associated with this property that Homer can actually refer to him in the first lines of the *Odyssey* using only his epithet, *polytropos*, without even giving his name in the full knowledge that listeners will know exactly who is meant. He is the man who is so deft in his use of language that in the blink of an eye he can catch up and entangle anyone in his web of words. The way in which Odysseus, at every step of the way during his long and adventurous life, is able to surmount every challenge which he encounters shows that he, more than anyone else, really instantiates the principle which he enunciates at the beginning of Sophocles' play: 'the tongue' is an even mightier weapon than the arm.

'His tongue', *glossa*: that literally is the word which Sophocles uses. The word *'glossa'* in Greek, as in English, designates the organ of speech, and it is thus distinguished from *logos*, which refers to the articulated, structured form of speech, to reason. According to Aristotle, 'nature does nothing in vain',[6] so every organ must by definition have a function. The organ of speech thus has as its function effective speaking, speech which leads to something. And speech is in fact often much more effective than mere over taction in actually getting things done. If 'energy' is power which can act, then speech, in the human world, is the supreme form of energy.

### Speech as tool. Eloquence, purely instrumental speech

Speech can function as a tool, a weapon, something which gets things done. For this reason, one obvious criterion to use in judging it is its effectiveness. This is the province of eloquence, the art of speaking well, that is, speaking so as to affect, touch, stir up, and move other people by using the techniques of rhetoric. This would include insulting them, offending them, hurting them, verbally knocking them out. According to a very influential view, one which has become more and more powerful over time and which now is the dominant one, eloquence has as its sole goal enhanced effectiveness. It considers speech to be an instrument to be used, deploying it as a means to an end, and the end is in one sense always the same: to persuade, convince, please, seduce. Traditional rhetoric distinguishes a number of different contexts within which speaking can occur, and a number of different appropriate local goals. Each of these contexts (and each of these goals) marks out a subgenre of eloquence: 'deliberative' eloquence has its home in discussions of how to act, and it tries to persuade people to engage in or abstain from some envisaged course of action. 'Judicial' eloquence is required in legal or court-related contexts and it attempts to help advocates defend or prosecute someone accused of a crime. 'Epideictic' or 'demonstrative' eloquence is concerned with praising or blaming in general. Eloquence, then, is an art aimed at achieving particular effects through the use of techniques to maximize the impact of words. As such, it should be an art based on a systematic knowledge of human behaviour, and it must itself be deployed as a subordinate part of a wider strategy which specifies what in each particular case the relevant context is and what local goal is to be attained.

In short, when speech is conceived as a tool, it is thought simply to be devoted to speaking well, not, that is, necessarily speaking in a way that is informed by and directed at the good in some general sense. A tool is neutral in that it does not itself determine the ends for which it is employed. It does not concern itself with that. A knife can be used to cut bread or to disembowel someone. Speech can praise a heroic person who performs memorable deeds of benevolence or it can allow a criminal to escape condign punishment. Considered merely as a tool, speech is neither good nor bad in itself. Its value depends on the ends for which it is used. Considered completely abstractly, eloquence is not *per se* a virtue, but rather its value depends on the sense we give it (or fail to give it) by using (or failing to use) it to advance some particular goal. To consider speech in this abstract way, as a pure tool, without assigning it any other vocation than its 'usefulness' is to deprive it of its moral dignity and cognitive standing, and eviscerate its sense. This is a way of neutralizing its humanity; by abstracting it from its organic connection with the rest of human life, speech is degraded and reduced to a mere mechanical lever which one can pull (or not) to produce particular effects.

*Lethal weapon. Capturing the public through speech*

If speech is reduced to its pragmatic use, treated merely as a tool, it can be put in the service of any cause whatever. There is a National Socialist eloquence, which drove whole populations mad by the force of its persuasiveness, and dev-astated the world. Once eloquence is cut free of the larger context of meaning in which it is embedded, it is free no longer to concern itself with *why* it is being used, that is, to what end; even less is it required to ask in *whose interest* it is deployed. This means that it is deprived of any reliable way of orienting itself globally. If that is the case, eloquence comes to be at the mercy of all the vicissitudes of fortune. If speech lacks the support provided by a humanistic framework and if it is not considered to be subject to moral evaluation, noth-ing stands in the way of treating the Other as a mere means and not an end-in-itself; not as a subject, and interlocutor, a potential *alter ego*, but as an object, a mere 'thing', a target for intervention. Speech prepares the way for conquest; it is an agent of domination.

So it should be no surprise that the prevailing conception of speech is that it is an instrument of domination. A speaker who 'takes the floor' in public is trying in some way to take control of the situation. Doing this deserves, I think, to be redescribed, using my own terms here, as attempting to 'cap-ture the public through speech'. 'Taking the floor' in order to speak is like 'taking power'. It is a way of trying to seize listeners, grab their attention, captivate them, hook them and reel them in, subjugate them. If Odysseus is right and speech governs the world, those who master speech will dominate the world, or, at any rate, *their* world, be it small or large. This is why all forms of 'leadership training' contain as a required component courses in public speaking. To be able to speak well is the Holy Grail of the True Leader, the Eldorado of lead-ership. In this sense at least, it is speech, not silence, which is worth its weight in gold. If that, however, is all speech is worth, compared to the infinite riches of humanity, it does not amount to very much. It all depends, then, on what one means by 'valuable'.

*Unless it is oriented to values, speech is a diminishing asset*

There can be little doubt but that speech creates values; that is one of its great inherent powers. However, when the public is 'captured by speech', the values in question are all passed through a filtering process, and they all end up being concentrated in one small domain. This filter is one imposed by strategic thinking and utilitarian calculation, and it operates by defining the values that are to be created in terms exclusively of interests, means available, goals, resources, results, conquests, costs, gains, losses, benefits, defeats, victories. After all, on this view, war is just economics pursued by other means; speech is monetarized and becomes just another commodity, something put in circulation with a view to being bought and sold on the market. It is something that takes place in a competitive, public arena, where it serves as a weapon on the field of battle which social interaction in our society has become. In fact, speech here is reduced to its pragmatic dimension, which is nothing but a shadow of itself, or to its superficial external appearance, and as such has only an instrumental role in action, as producing a certain practical effect. Speech which has been 'operationalized' in this way has no value but its usefulness, and recognizes no value apart from that of its own effectiveness.

This is the conception of speech one finds in the speeches of the ancient Sophists, a conception which Plato denounces in his dialogue the *Gorgias*, or, as the subtitle provided by the ancient editors has it, *On Rhetoric*. Rhetoric, Socrates holds, is nothing but a mask for sophistry, a Weapon of Mass Persuasion with a simple credo: people can be persuaded of *anything*. Speech has the power to do anything, and this power depends for support on nothing apart from itself. It is the Alpha and Omega of everything; it is not subject to evaluation in any framework other than that which it itself provides, and the only criterion for assessing it is its effectiveness. There are no higher values for judging it; in fact, strictly speaking, no values at all, no good or bad, no justice or injustice, no beauty or deformity, no truth or falsehood. All that exist are discourses which oppose each other, and prevail (or not) by virtue of the power they exercise. If, to illustrate what truth is, I say that 'a human being' is 'a two-legged animal without feathers', a Sophist will pluck a chicken and say that this is what I mean by 'a human being'[7] and I will have lost the encounter. It is not the 'truth' which carries the day – 'truth' does not exist. It is the most powerful speech which wins out. A point is scored or lost in an exchange; there is nothing more.

In opposition to the relativism of the Sophists, Socrates inaugurates a quest, the quest by philosophy for that which is essential. The 'philosophy' which he envisaged was to be a search for the truth which proceeds by asking about the goals of life, tries to determine what is really valuable, gives orientation to action, works at attaining the good, especially the good life; all this in the service of realizing humanity. 'What do you call "thinking"?' Theaetetus asks, and Socrates replies: 'A dialogue of the soul with itself.'[8] Arising out of dialogue and advancing through successive stages of reflective thinking (which is, as we have seen, a kind of internal dialogue), philosophy never stops obsessing about the real meaning of speech. Why do we speak? To what end? In whose interest? What does speech presuppose? What are its implications? What is it immediately aimed at? To what does it commit me? To whom am I speaking? Who is speaking when I talk? And when I do talk, what do I mean to say? The view that the use of language is to 'capture the public through speech' is a massive error. It reduces speech to eloquence and eloquence to a sheerly instrumental virtue. It is a mistake to consider language only in terms of its utility, as something which can then be evaluated from a merely technical point of view. This can easily turn into a kind of technological fundamentalism, as if the existence of technology rendered thought superfluous. In fact, we need an even higher level of reflection to compensate for the reductive tendency inherent in our obsession with gadgetry. This approach neglects the philosophical substratum of speech – the only thing which is capable of allowing us to imagine what it is to be human in the fullest sense. The great illusion here is that of trying only to capture the public by speech, because this encourages us to remain on the surface of things. It is a mistake to focus only on the means speech uses and the effects it has, without fully entering into the complex world composed of the reasons for speaking and the ultimate goals speech is trying to achieve. And yet, from the point of view of those to whom speech is directed, it is precisely this nexus of reasons and goals which will, finally, be most important. When someone is addressing me, what is it, in them, that is really speaking to me?

*Speech as a holistic fact about humanity.*
*Putting an end to 'speech is a tool'*

Speaking is an engagement of the whole person, of our spirit, our heart, our body, and our soul; of our impulses, our emotions, our will, our reason. It is a holistic fact about us, the expression of our singular existence, which causes all the parts of us to resonate together, and can cause 'sympathetic resonance' in all parts of the person to whom we speak. To mutilate speech is to truncate our humanity. Speech suffers an amputation and loses its noblest and most attractive feature if it is divided up mechanically, limited to its most superficial tasks, cut off from its profound human context, turned into something merely functional, and detached from its long-term field of action. This is why eloquence is not enough. As I have said, what we must do is to say that which is good, not merely speak 'well'. We need, that is, to try to articulate the common good, which means speaking correctly and justly, with discernment and attention, good sense and responsibility. All of this requires something more than just an art of rhetorical eloquence; it requires a philosophy of speech, which is the only way of integrating all the dimensions of our human existence, rendering them coherent, encouraging them to coexist fruitfully, and rendering their necessities consistent. This includes all domains of our existence from metaphysics to poetics, from logic to aesthetics, from ethics to politics, from what-we-are to what-we-can-create, from thought to its expression, from attention to interpretation, from interaction to integration. Our goal should be to align our speech properly and to live our lives accordingly. Speech that is well aligned in the sense envisaged here would penetrate all the parts of our existence, expressing all its aspects while linking us intimately with our plans. It would operate in such a way that in its action all our faculties – reason, the will, the imagination – would overlap and cooperate, and in so doing speech would articulate and advance our highest aspirations. Such speech would aid reason in its search for the truth, make it easier for the will to assume responsibility for action, and stimulate the imagination in its pursuit of beauty.

We are not preaching the doctrine that 'speech should be without a specific organ', echoing, as it were, Antonin Artaud, who in 'To Have Done with the Judgment of God' called for the creation of a 'body without organs' which would finally be freed of all its 'automatic reactions' and restored to its 'true freedom'.[9] Our goal is to get beyond the idea of speech as a tool, as a particular organ of which we make use, in order to give it back its full sense and meaning. We start with our sense of the Other.

# 2

# The Other does not exist

### The end of the Other. Humanity in pieces

*The Society of Transmission*

Our time is the Age of Transmission. It makes a cult of broadcasting, disseminating, propagating whatever the cost. This is the era of the 'buzz', when things 'go viral'. That really says it all. The highest aspiration of a message is to mutate and transform itself into a virus, that is, something like a contagious disease, to change the inherent rhythm that governs the circulation of proper, substantial messages among hearers and speakers, and replace it with the attempt to maximize the speed of propagation. To increase at all costs the number of 'hits', to have an impact that grows exponentially, eventually to expand explosively like a supernova and attain universal hegemony. This is the pattern which a highly infectious virus exhibits, that is, it becomes something against which there is no defence, something which cannot be controlled, something which is almost invariably harmful, and sometimes fatal. The message, like a virus, propagates itself, even when the hosts are unaware of it, reproducing versions of itself without end, until it exhausts the natural resources on which it depends,

but by that time it will have destroyed its original hosts completely and moved on to others, which it will also ravage. In
the film *The Matrix*, Agent Smith, who is a part of the program
specifically designed to defend the Matrix against disruption,
describes the human species itself in exactly these terms: it
is a 'plague', a 'cancer of this planet', a 'disease', a 'virus' that
disturbs the 'natural equilibrium with the surrounding environment' and destroys its harmony.[1] After all, all by itself a
single electronic virus can paralyse a whole network. In our
contemporary societies – all of them societies of continual
and fluctuating transmission – the logic of virulence has con-
taminated almost all forms of transmitting information, and
it has done so to such an extent that it affects all our interactions, and even poisons our personal relations. The Society of
Transmission turns out to be one which tries to dispense with
'society' altogether.

In this new social formation, the goal is to make as much of
an impression as possible. This is why there is such a focus on
the sheer number of 'hits' the message receives (rather than
on the Others who form the potential audience). The message is shaped to have maximal impact on the target audience,
not to initiate any kind of exchange or interaction with them.
'Feedback' is a tool engineered to optimize the effectiveness of
the program set up to transmit the message. It is perhaps no
accident that the members of the target audience are called
'users', just as drug addicts are, that is, deeply dependent,
passive consumers. The only form of pseudo-activity left to
them is the lame and pitiful 'Feedback', which gives them at
most the illusion of having a voice and a right to speak. This
is the only way for them to prevent themselves from being
driven mad when they see themselves constantly objectified
and transformed into a bit of computer data. 'Interactivity' is
a Potemkin village that hides the ruins of dialogue behind its
slick façades.

Transmitting is not conversing; it is one-way speech

which imposes an asymmetry on any exchange. It shunts speech off onto a side-track which leads to a dead-end, and prevents meaning from circulating freely. It can cause a fatal obstruction in social relations when one party tries to pour out everything that is on their mind and make everyone else accept it all. This is bad for everyone, even for the mono-maniacal 'Broadcaster' who dominates all the available space, leaving no room for others to think or express themselves: that person, too, gets nothing from the interaction. They are merely squandering their own substance, like an organism which always rejects external nourishment and never ingests anything. The Broadcaster is like someone always breathing out without ever breathing in. They embark on a one-way trip from which they never come back and on which no other ever returns to them.

## *What is missing? Listening*

People don't listen to each other any more. No one cares – and why care anyway? They also don't speak *to*, but *at*, each other. This is the exact opposite of speech in the true sense. We address each other as if we were shouting at a blank wall, but even walls have ears. Media training sessions make a point of teaching one how not to listen. It goes without saying that one need never answer a question. Whatever anyone says to you, just trumpet your own message, loud and clear. Then repeat it five times to hammer it into the brain of every member of the audience. These are your talking points; your handlers have pre-masticated them for you; all you need to do is spit them out. Don't hesitate to do it again and again. However, since the interviewers themselves often don't bother to listen, the whole thing degenerates into mere noise – no one is actually speaking to anyone. Politicians are no better than media people: they interrupt each other in exchanges that are no more than verbal assaults. At best they are digging parallel tunnels through the hard rock; at worst it is mutual assured destruction. To speak of a 'dialogue of the deaf' in cases like this would be an insult to those who have difficulty hearing because they, after all, generally pay very careful attention to what is being said around them. Employers don't listen to their employees because they think they 'know already what *those* people will say'. The employees return the favour because, after all, 'The bosses couldn't really understand me anyway. That's OK, I know what I have to do.' Co-workers don't listen to each other: 'Those guys in the next department don't have a clue; it's a mess over there, but I know what they ought to do.' Parents don't listen to their children: 'But that's not true, Dad, you always go blank when I'm talking to you.' Even couples do not always listen to each other: 'Sorry, dear, could you say that again?' – 'But, darling, I've already told you three times.'

## Capturing the Other

Broadcasting is what it is all about. This is the world of 'LOL', where the highest compliment is 'This video will blow you away!'; where humor, commentary, response, and reaction are reduced to placing the emoticon of a little heart or a sad face next to a tweet. And where the ultimate praise for a put-down is: 'This post is a killer.' One must broadcast without considering the Other – except as a *target*. The Others are what I take aim at. They are objects – the objects of my observation or of my research; or of my seduction, or objects to be plundered or even destroyed. Icons, clients, prey, potential booty, enemies. The Others become simply something to seduce or to reject. Their value consists in nothing but what they might bring me; they are a mere means to increase my real or symbolic capital: the number of hits on my site, the number of 'likes' my tweets attract, the number of retweets I can amass. The question is what can I get from them. They are the ones who give me or deprive me of my status as an 'influencer', the recognition I enjoy, my celebrity, my prestige and standing. The 'buzz' generated by my posts increases my ratings, which in turn eventually brings in more money. This is a manipulative attitude which relates to the Other in an exclusively strategic or commercial way, as someone to douse with advertising campaigns and vanquish.

## The abolition of the Other

In this ferocious war, the first thing is to get the Other's attention. In fact, this obsession with the fact that others are staring at me is basically the expression of an attitude of total indifference, of complete lack of interest in them – 'Who cares about them?'; 'What they think doesn't interest me at all' – because fundamentally for me they are scarcely more than potential objects of one of my charm offensives. They are not interlocutors; none is a potential *alter ego* engaged in an interpersonal exchange; instead each one is just one more thing-like object. In this vanity fair of objects, where are the Others as subjects? Who really cares about them? How are they hearing what I say to them? How does it resonate with them? How do I take account of and make room for their reactions, their responses, their silence? How do I understand what is only implicit in them? In short, what is happening between us when we interact subject-to-subject? For any kind of encounter or interaction to take place, there must be at least two subjects. A thousand emoticons cannot ever replace one emotion.

'With words one man can make another blessed, or drive him to despair,' writes Freud.[2] A single word can kill; there can be no doubt about that. To see that this is true one need only look at all those people – children, adolescents, adults – who suffer from electronic bullying. Insulted, humiliated, stigmatized, worn down, bombarded with hateful messages, savaged on the internet, tracked down mercilessly and held up to unceasing ridicule, they see their world collapse, their lives destroyed, and themselves degraded – a torment that sometimes ends in suicide. Not everything that can be said is good to say – even less is it good to hear. Not all speech is inherently good. This holds in spades when the speaker has no regard for the Other, does not take them into account at all as a person, and does not recognize their humanity. There is no reciprocity in any exchange, no subtlety in the positions taken, no nuance in anything, no apparent awareness of complexity. When speech like this is unleashed, it is like a time bomb left to explode in a murderous outburst.

The logic of this commitment to expression at any cost, in which each speaker competes with all the others in covering themselves more and more outrageously with the alibi provided by the sacrosanct principle of 'free speech', ends in universal destruction. As if there could be such a thing as freedom without any limits. 'Liberty consists in the power to do whatever does not harm anyone else.' The *Declaration of the Rights of Man and of the Citizen* stipulates this principle as the foundation of the rule of law right from the start in its Article 4. Conversely, unlimited liberty is a state of despotism. As Hegel says, it is a world where only one person is free.[3] Because only a despot really enjoys unlimited liberty, and never encounters any boundaries to that freedom marked out by the liberty of others. The despot is 'free' in the sense that they have total power over others who are themselves completely unfree. This is the dizzying paradox that Dostoevsky formulates when he writes in *The Possessed:* 'Starting from unlimited freedom, I arrive at unlimited despotism.'[4]

### The culture of humiliation

If one can say literally anything, this also means that one can destroy anything. That is the way social networks operate. If the Other does not really exist, all is permitted. This is how the

Kingdom of Irresponsible Speech gets established; how it gives its blessing to forms of speech that arise when people simply let themselves go, without measure, without restraint, without limits. Actually, what we need is the exact reverse of that: we need to take the measure of the words we use. We need to dig in and claw our way back up the slippery slope down which we are sliding. Because if it is true that our era is devoted to the cult of Broadcasting, it is also ineluctably fated to nourish a culture of humiliation. Since what we are trying to do is understand what it is to speak today, as part of that enterprise we need to evaluate speech morally. Then at least one thing becomes immediately clear about speech in our electronically interconnected world: the massive orgasmic pleasure taken in inflicting systematic humiliation, in repeatedly seeking out people to hound and put definitively beyond the pale, and in throwing them to the dogs. These are forms of evil. It is the evil Nietzsche describes in *The Gay Science* when he writes:

*Whom do you call bad?* – Those who always want to put to shame.

*What do you consider most humane?* – To spare someone shame.

*What is the seal of liberation?* – No longer being ashamed in front of oneself.[5]

This ethics is a world away from the *Name and Shame* culture which flourishes now, a culture that thrives on denouncing people to humiliate them and 'exposing' them to destroy them. There is, of course, nothing wrong with denouncing evil – that is perfectly legitimate and necessary, even salutary – but to condemn evil by arbitrarily inflicting unwarranted public humiliation on people, without any real need or just for the sake of amusement, as an exercise in cruelty or from some insalubrious inner compulsion, is another thing altogether. It is even worse than this because sometimes the joint effect of the herd instinct and the hyperbole to which modern media are prone is to generate something that borders on mass hysteria. Then the humiliation which is meted out is so extreme that it resembles a massacre of the innocent. In discussing this, one must never overlook, minimize, or deny that relations of power, force, and domination are at play here. Nor must one throw doubt on the fact that the agents involved in this kind of persecution are genuinely culpable, nor minimize the gravity of the crimes they commit. We find ourselves stuck in a surreal phantasmagoria: in the middle of a spillway that channels off the overflow from a enormous reservoir of musty effluents, surrounded on all sides by fast-flowing streams of verbal violence and murderous invective ('all just for fun'). It's a battle to the death with tweets and posts that create buzz as weapons, and where only the one who Broadcasts lives, and only the one who has the sharpest elbows and the quickest reflexes to crush the Other can survive. What we really need to do is find a way out of here.

## The triumph of the cliché.
## Individuals reduced to stereotypes

### The theatre of stereotypes

That is the reason we need to get rid of the set of stereotypes that dominates modern society. We need to reacquaint ourselves with complexity, nuance, subtlety, the benevolence of a genuine exchange of views and the life-saving distance which humour generates, and we need to reintegrate them into our lives. This means, in particular, putting an end to the systematic reduction of our identities to a handful of clichés. 'Are you a Victim or a Bastard? An Accomplice or a Hero? A Public Prosecutor or an Executioner? None of these? Well, then at least you are a Witness, aren't you? Is the answer still "no"?

That's impossible, you have to be *something*.' Note that this is not a slip of the tongue: 'some*thing*' not 'some*one*'. Welcome to an era in which there is a pigeon-hole for everyone.

In dramatic terms, we have been brought down to the absolute rock bottom, or even to a level below that: what we have is the bare minimum needed for there to be any drama at all. From the crisis in the health services to the presidential campaign, from the various artificially inflated major political 'affairs' to the smallest article in the daily newspaper, you can sum up public debate in the media as a series of skits, each one featuring only seven main characters, each one of these a cliché. There is the Victim, the Bastard, the Accomplice, the Hero, the Public Prosecutor, the Executioner, and the Witness. These same seven characters are constantly invoked as if they were enough to *dramatize* any issue of public concern. 'Dramatize' in a two-fold sense: first, as if any issue could be understood by reference to a plot in which only these seven archetypical characters figure, manoeuvring and conducting intrigues against each other; and, second, as if the best way to gain the public's attention is to present things like this, accentuating the dramatic element in the confrontation.

### Bare-bones drama

These, then, are the four laws that govern our political debate: reduction of everything to stereotypes; the imperative to put each actor in a single pre-determined pigeon-hole; the illusion that individuals have a choice about which role to adopt, whereas in fact they have a role imposed on them; and the obligatory use of a minimum fixed set of stock figures by means of which any event can be fit into a pre-given schema for presentation in the media.

1. *Universal formatting.* Our most powerful collectives – the state, the media, public opinion, social networks – operate by negating the individual, reducing it to a single dimension, and

assigning it a standardized identity. In fact, what I say or do, or what I actually am, are irrelevant once I am fixed and my individuality is denied, crushed, and *obliterated* in this way – once I find myself made into a specimen with a single-word description hung around my neck. For instance, the moment any expert on Covid said anything in public, they were tagged as being 'reassuring' or 'alarmist'. Human complexity is the enemy; singularity a danger; conformity to a standard model a form of security. As a result, we all become stereotypes.

2. *The categorical imperative.* The new categorical imperative of our society is that each of us must see our identity as fitting into one of the categories imposed on us. The available roles are limited and all sharply defined, and they are assigned on a mass basis. Whole swathes of people are summarily put into one category and locked in there. For instance, are we, the French, in this era of Covid 66 million public prosecutors or 66 million victims? Everyone is one or the other. The result: we are all seen, each one of us, as part of a monolith.

3. *The imposition of one's role.* Liberty consists merely in being able to choose one uniform from the given pile. Pick your camp, comrade. Better still, put on your costume; you are a *follower.* Make yourself fit in with the script. Get into your appropriate little box. Melt yourself down into the person you are destined to be, the label you've been given, the cliché that defines you. Since, as Emmanuel Macron said, 'we are at war' (at that moment against Covid, but there is always another war), you are all heroes; this constant refrain assigns you a role definitively. Anyway, in times of crisis, discourse must be radicalized and discussion prohibited. The result: we are all just reduced to stereotypes.

4. *The logic of quotas.* (a) A fact enters the mainstream only if it plays along in the game of the seven stereotypes. (b) For the media, even to exist, an event has to be presented as exhibiting at least three of the seven stereotypes. Without this minimum, it will remain invisible. (c) It is never the case that just two of

the stereotypes are deployed; if two are there, a third will be spontaneously generated to give the dramatic action a boost. For instance, in a recent British case, when the Bastards in the Post Office confronted their Victims, the accused Sub-Postmasters, this confrontation itself generated the need for the intervention of a Hero, Sir Alan Bates. The result: we are all antagonists in an ongoing struggle.

### The seven deadly clichés

There is, then, a dramatic structure which determines how information and news are formatted and presented to us nowadays. At its heart are seven stereotypes, seven roles that must be filled for some event to become part of our National History. Citizens of France! One more effort and you will be able to make yourselves into stock characters.

1. *The Bastard* defiles everything he touches. He is a living horror, a cesspit of vices and cruelty. '*Chaque instant de [s]a vie est chargé de souillures/ Elle n'est qu'un amas de crimes et d'ordures* [Every moment of his life is filthy/ It is nothing but a mass of crimes and muck]' (*Tartuffe*).[6] He is a man of violence, a rapist, who abuses, corrupts, destroys. He is intoxicated with the sense of his own omnipotence, and does whatever he needs to do to satisfy his basest impulses, committing crimes without compunction. He seems to enjoy complete immunity; for a while at least – a long time, even a very long time – because he has protection. It is, in the first instance, his power that pro-tects him, but also his reputation for ruthlessness, the alliances he has formed, the system of subordinates he has created to insulate himself from attack, his wealth, his arrogance. He has a proper court with clients, hangers-on, henchmen. He is also surrounded by a silent wall of *omertà*. Like the young Michael Corleone in *The Godfather*,[7] without scruples or empathy, he violates all the principles he publicly professes. What his life amounts to is domination, the perversion of all that is good,

and devastation on all sides. He puts his own satisfaction above all else. The emotions he provokes are fascination and repulsion in equal part.

2. *The Victim* is defined by suffering, by the shock of a life occluded and ruined. 'Pain marks you, but too deep to see' (says June, a sex slave in *The Handmaid's Tale* who lives in a totalitarian and misogynist fascist state).[8] The pain never goes away. The Victim suffers for all time from the torment the Bastard inflicts. Fatally wounded and impaired for life, still the Victim hides her trauma, which eats away at her from within. In a perverse reversal of all that is natural, she can even come to feel guilty, as if she were responsible for the horror she has had to endure. She knows: the Bastard will never forgive her for the evil he has visited upon her. She will spend the rest of her life *afterwards* struggling against the horrible things which were done to her and which still blight her existence: against violence, suffering, humiliation, solitude. She puts survival above all else, and provokes our compassion.

3. *The Accomplice* provides cover. He is the master of accommodation, connivance, complicity – but what he deserves is to be covered with shame. 'Thank God the statute of limitations now applies to these actions' (according to a statement by Cardinal Barbarin on the paedophilic crimes committed in his archbishopric by one of his priests). The Accomplice is a major stake-holder in the enterprise of which the Bastard is the principal actor. His stake may be based on his friendship with the Bastard, or on self-interest, cowardice, or corruption. He and the Bastard belong to the same world and live in the same milieu. Athough he is part of a reprehensible organization, he sits around cultivating his silence and organizing ways in which he can 'fail to notice' things, so that he can wash his hands in innocence. If he is called to account by the victim, it is always the case that he knew nothing. That is, it turns out, he did actually know, but he didn't trust the evidence, or didn't dare to say anything or he couldn't say

anything, or he didn't have the right to say anything. And anyway a suspect is innocent until proven guilty, isn't he? And one must not rock the boat, one must keep up appearances, avoid scandal, and defend the institution. The emotion he evokes is disgust.

4. *The Witness* reveals the truth. The revelations are explosive and cause scandal. 'Villainy, villainy, villainy! ... 'Twill out, 'twill out. I, peace! No, I will speak as liberal as the north' (Emilia revealing to Othello the fatal treachery of his 'faithful' Iago).[9] The Witness cannot take it any more. She is horrified and overwhelmed by the silent suffering of the victim, and as a last resort she denounces the Bastard, revealing his wicked deeds. The Witness proclaims out loud the suffering which the Bastard has caused, in order that the truth, so long silenced, may at last be heard, justice done, and there be an end to impunity from punishment. The great fear the Victim felt should now come to haunt the Bastard. Despite the length of time elapsed, finally, even at this late date, the Victim can speak. What is most important is that the truth be brought to light. The emotion this provokes is sympathy.

5. *The Public Prosecutor* issues an indictment. Her realm is that of indignation and condemnation. Someone will be burned at the stake. 'Rights? Someone like you has no rights. Kill him,' say the gangsters who have constituted themselves a People's Tribunal in Fritz Lang's *M*.[10] The Public Prosecutor is indignant; she rails, she accuses, she reproves, she castigates, she berates. She is a Grand Inquisitor whose first reflex is to attack and condemn, and she does so on principle. She does not do things 'by the book'; she 'throws the book' at the Bastard. Because *she knows*. She has seen it in black and white on Twitter (now known as 'X'), so it must be true. The proof: it is shown again and again in a continuous loop on the internet. So she expresses her disgust, her revulsion. She *annihilates* all the bastards – except those on her own network. Mess them up good, that's it. The emotion she provokes: anger.

6. *The Executioner* is the oppressor *par excellence*. The agent of torture, the right-hand man of any dictatorship. His symbol is the wound: 'If you want a picture of the future, imagine a boot stamping on a human face – for ever' (one of the maxims of the thought police in George Orwell's *1984*).[11] He is the one who wields the whip. He is obsessed with domination and control, and operates by producing terror with the goal of perpetuating himself and the regime he serves. He is the reality of the police state. The truth he embodies is that of tyranny and infamy. His method is to keep those in his purview under surveillance and punish them. His great pleasure: to keep people subjugated and make them suffer. His first reflex: to wield his baton and issue prohibitions. His final resort: liquidating people or allowing them to die. He has the arrogance of his privileged position and an impudence which results from having a good conscience. His three traits: he crushes dignity, humanity, and responsibility. It is quite right to rise up against him: he would crush everything. When one side says, 'Down with the police state!' the other replies, 'Long live oppression!' The emotion the Executioner provokes is hatred.

7. *The Hero* saves the day. Her characteristics are devotion and willingness to push herself beyond her own limits; she is the one capable of genuine self-sacrifice. 'I volunteer as tribute!' (Katniss Everdeen says in *The Hunger Games* as she offers to take the place of her younger sister to save her from certain death).[12] The hero takes up the struggle on the behalf of someone else, exposes herself to danger, gives her own life, all the while demonstrating her own extreme courage and selflessness. She is the first to confront a crisis, try to deal with a catastrophe, make war, even if she is not in the front line. She sacrifices self to save her country, defend her homeland, serve her nation. She holds nothing back. Whatever happens – catastrophe, terrorism, pandemic – she holds herself upright in the face of history and in the face of all the other people in the world, even if they were to forget her on the very first day of

the world 'after' the crisis. She will not give up, no matter what the cost. She puts the salvation of the Other above all else, and provokes the emotion of admiration.

These are the seven major clichés that dominate the debate in our media today. Much less captivating than the seven age-old deadly sins of our ancestors, but just as canonical and inescapable for us as they were, because of what they impose on us. They propound a simple classification of human beings and a simple structure for possible courses of action. Some ways of acting are definitively 'in' (for some people); some are just as definitively 'out'. The struggle between individuals and groups is less open here than that between the five mafia families in *The Godfather*. The classification is also less juicy than that offered in *The Good, the Bad and the Ugly*, where one of the characters wittily suggests: 'In this world, there's two kinds of people, my friend: those with loaded guns and those who dig. You dig.'[13] Structurally the stories are, however, equally simple.

## *We need to reactivate the spirit of complexity*

No, to be serious, our world is not divided exclusively into seven categories. Unless we are willing to accept that one size must always fit all, and everything must conform to some pre-given stereotypes, in which individuality is crushed and only categories remain. This text is an attempt to argue for multiple identities, and to defend the infinity multiplication of possible interpretations. I wish to speak out against radical reductionism, against the gradual erasure of individual differences until things fit smoothly into a scale along only one dimension. What is at risk here is nothing less than our freedom, our singularity, our truth. Our humanity. The question now is to what extent we are even capable any more of inventing ourselves and not simply making the summary judgement that we belong in one or the other of these small pigeon holes. How can we tell our own story and write our own history rather than having it

imposed on us from outside? How can we choose to be ourselves as people always in the process of becoming something
else, in the flux of life?

To do this, we need to adopt again what Milan Kundera calls
that 'wisdom of uncertainty' which refuses 'the din of easy,
quick answers that come faster than the question and block it
off'. We need to return to the 'spirit of complexity' which tells
us: 'Things are not as simple as you think.'[14] Being a human is
also more complicated. That is why I reject the clichés derived
from central casting, and wish to propose here a general, over-
arching way of seeing the drama of human life which takes
account of its complexity. We need to develop an art which
allows us to narrate the story of our own epoch while doing
justice to its multitudinous variety, an art that lets us listen and
be attentive to others, while remaining self-aware.

# 3

# Subject not at home

## Welcome to Zombieland

### *The ethics of reciprocity*

Speech itself demands that it be heard and listened to by others. It is the art of the Other. From its point of view, the difference between people is a foundational fact about humanity. To be is to be in the world, and that means with other people. *With* – not *against* and much less *without* – people. That is why speech, if it is understood in its proper sense, and correctly and sensibly undertaken and executed, is at the heart of humanism. There is a virtuous circularity here in that correct speech presupposes, but also generates and fosters, a responsible relation with the Other, one founded on the moral principle often called 'The Golden Rule': 'Do not do to others what you do not want them to do to you.'[1] This rule is accepted by a wide range of religions and ethical systems, from Zoroastrianism to Confucianism and from Taoism to the various kinds of monotheism, and it has been taken to be a cardinal principle of morality by Western thinkers from the authors of the Bible to Immanuel Kant. In its active version, it reads: 'Do unto others as you would have others do unto you.'[2] Kant reformulates it as never treat others simply as a means to an end, but also as ends-in-themselves. Not as mere objects, but as your own image and likeness.[3]

In this sense, speech implies an ethics of reciprocity: I listen to you as you speak; you listen to me as I speak. We speak to each other, *ergo* we exist. Part of that existence is a desire for equilibrium in the interaction, for a constant rebalancing in our relation to the Other. To listen is to open a space for the Other, and give them the liberty to be and say what they wish. It can even be seen as a way of offering them a field of action in which a new form of freedom is possible: the freedom of interaction. By speaking and listening I can confer on them the status of a fully recognized being, giving them an existence in me, but as someone other than me. I can take account of them rather than simply treating them as if they counted for nothing.

### The value of attention

There is an excellent name for this process: it is called 'attention'. To pay attention to someone is at the same time to listen to them and to respect them. The word 'regard' has an appropriate ambiguity: to *look* at them *and* to hold them in a certain esteem. There is a more strictly cognitive dimension (perceiving what the Other has to say) and a more strictly moral one (giving consideration to what they say). Paying attention to someone is taking in what they say and giving it the space and the weight it deserves. To show that I am genuinely paying attention to others, I need to give them the consideration that is their due, that is, I need to treat each one as a potential *alter ego*.

Speech demands attention, the capacity to take in and give consideration to what the Other says in the present instant, at the very moment in which the conversation is taking place. Attention is an activity; it mobilizes my whole being, involves my body, and engages my consciousness. The Latin etymology of the word gets it right: it is literally a matter of 'straining toward' (*ad* + *tendere*). When I pay attention, my mind is straining toward that which it is attending to: toward the Other and what they say. This is a strenuous process.

## The tyranny of distraction

The effort which attention demands of us seems each day more difficult to muster, because our capacity to pay attention has already been so enormously eroded. The reason for this is the joint effect of a number of diverse but extremely powerful dynamic factors which have converged. Each of these has contributed to preventing us from stepping out of the continual flux of new information and opinion that surrounds us and simply pausing to settle down at rest with and in ourselves, even for a moment. Together these factors exert overwhelming pressure on us. The elements that come together to create this situation include: the sheer astronomical amount of information that inundates us and the vertiginous acceleration of the speed at which it is thrust on us; the context-less, chaotic way in which facts are made to flash by us; the tyranny which the cult of the 'new' exercises; the extreme planned obsolescence which is built into so many features of our world – no sooner has something appeared for the first time than it is already *passé*; and the dictatorial hegemony of speed and immediacy together with a concomitant radicalization of impatience. In a world like this, exasperation becomes universal. In fact, a titanic war is being conducted against us to capture our attention – the mental time we have available – in order to sell it to the highest bidder. The many offers of a 'free' this-or-that are just so many cons: 'If it's free, you are the product on offer.' We are bombarded with notifications and suffocated under an avalanche of solicitations. We are saturated with stimuli which constantly interrupt us and systematically interfere with our capacity to focus. We are also expected to reply instantaneously to everything – immediately, all the time. Extreme forms of surfing on the multiplicity of channels now available mean that multitasking has become our default position, and enforced distraction our natural state. That is why we seem to be surrounded by people who stand or walk with their heads down as they gaze distractedly with their noses glued to a tiny screen and frantically scroll away – we are effectively walking zombies. That is the way we navigate our way through life, glassy-eyed, absent to ourselves and the world around us – off in a daze, elsewhere. It all rushes past, nothing stays fixed, nothing stays in place. We are mere bits of straw blown around in the wind, at the mercy of the flux, buffeted by every passing storm – without memory, without roots, without a horizon.

'What a life! Real life is absent. We are not in the world.'[4] That is the modern form of hell – but without its own Rimbaud. Rimbaud spoke of 'the alchemy of the word', but our world is governed by mere fluid dynamics. Constantly pumped full of liquid information against our wills, we no longer have the space, the energy, the flexibility, the capacity to accept any more. No power; no space; no time. We're closed down.


*Permanent saturation*

Making a space in which to take in and accept the Other, however, demands at least a minimum of freedom and recep-tiveness, of being open for business. Receptiveness is another word for listening, and as such as a condition of attention. Most of the time, though, we are not even present and open to ourselves, and so how could we be receptive to the Other? But we need to make a place in ourselves to receive them, create a mode of access which will allow them to enter our space. We need to pull ourselves up out of the billowing waves of distracting irrelevant stimuli so that an island can emerge on which an encounter would be possible. We need to raise a dyke to prevent inundation so a small patch of land can become visible, and stop the unrelenting flow of ever more information in its course so that we experience a moment of repose. We need to exit from the universal noise and learn to be able to remain silent.

Speech cannot ring out except against the background of silence. Without a background of silence, words can have no resonance. Without receptiveness, no words can be heard. Without attention, there can be no relations between people. So we need as a matter of urgency to change the structure of speaking in our society. We need to move on from treating speech as a pure individual attempt at attaining some end and see that it must also include giving the Other our full attention. And one must not be deceived about which of the two —performative expression or close attention – is the more active, productive, and beneficial. It is not the one you might antecedently think, and the reason for that is that, as far as speech is concerned, it is precisely the demand that all parties pay careful attention which enhances performance. In fact, it is the idolatry of 'effectiveness' which actually ruins attention.

## The addiction to stimuli

Speech in the proper sense makes demands on our time. It does not just require that we *have* time, but also that we *take* our time. Because paying attention to something means striving toward it, that is, engaging oneself in a present which is actively focused on the thing in question, and this active engagement must last for the whole period during which one's concentration is required. We need to focus intensely on what is being said – here and now – and concentrate on the way in which the whole process of speaking and listening works itself out: from the first word to the last silence.

The civilizational change which we are experiencing now is one that has produced a corresponding change in our relation to time. We have lost the ability to wait patiently; we no longer take the time to pay attention. We have no tolerance of boredom. We want everything immediately – *chop-chop*. Each instant is supposed to bring us a high, a new shock from new information; every notification must be like the rush of a drug in the bloodstream. Each moment must come with its own tiny frisson, its small charge of stimulation, and discharge, and its little satisfaction. Now, suddenly, we find we are hooked – frankly we're addicted to the atomization of our time, the constant succession of new hits, the fragmentation of speech. Our whole world is segmented into a series of 'capsules' – tiny pills or huge structures mounted on rockets. The drugs are free and we'll even throw in a nuclear missile without further charge; all we want in return is *you*. The more noise the whole thing makes, the bigger the splash. This is the way things are in the Kingdom of Messages: clichés, memes, acronyms, slogans, reels, the dust to which words return when they die – everywhere. The 'message' is in every case reduced to the simplest expressive fragment – nothing that one could even call an 'idea', just an image, at best a sketch. Ten seconds? Too long, try for five. The briefer the better. Think 'stimulus'. Your messaging must be brief, intense, repetitive, catchy, irresistible.

The 'speech' I am proposing is, on the contrary, a kind that lives, breathes, and unfolds in time.

### In praise of presence. The present moment of life

Speech demands presence just as much as time does. What is 'presence'? As the name implies, it is basically the ability to be *here* – rather than somewhere else. It is the way in which listening gives itself real corporeal existence, and as such the exact opposite of the state in which one's attention is wandering. I am fully present when I mobilize all my power of concentration and engagement on all dimensions: the physical, the psychic, the emotional, the intellectual. All aspects of me as a person must be involved, and I must be able to integrate all my faculties: body and soul, heart and spirit. To be present in the full sense is to be present to oneself, to the world, and to the Other. This is how I become fully real and manifest my full vitality. It is what gives external substance to what I think and mean; it makes what is essential to me a matter of flesh and blood.

It is no accident that many age-old philosophies and forms of wisdom – Buddhism, Yoga, Stoicism, and so forth – although they arose under very different historical and geographical circumstances, share a common concern with a question which they all think is crucial: how can I succeed in becoming fully *here*, fully *present* – fully *in* the present and *open to* the present? Always present at this moment and in this moment? It is also no accident that in both French and English, and also in other languages, the word 'present' is used both for what one offers to another as a gift and for the current moment. The present is the gift of this moment. What it offers us is the chance to live now in this instant. In contrast, the past, as Camus writes,[5] is that which no longer exists, just as the future is that which does not yet exist – the only things that exist are the present and the human body. Or, following Augustine,[6] one could say that all that exists is the present of the present (direct intuition), the present of the past (memory), and the present of the future (expectation) – all of these times are contained within the unique present of my consciousness. From the body to consciousness, the present is the time of my physical presence.

## Relationships in ruins. Welcome to a world of irreality

### *The society of screens*

Speech is an art of the present moment and of physical presence. These are all the more vital in a haunted age which is populated by people looking at each other with glassy stares through lenses, filters, and screens, by disembodied aliases, and by anonymous, absent subscribers. It is striking how difficult it has become to speak to another real human being. If you ring, you will most likely get a machine, a bot, a recorded message, or an automated answering service. *No person ever answers.*[7] On the other hand, to say of someone that they have great 'presence' means to emphasize a fact about them which has become increasingly rare, namely that they are invariably *completely there* in any encounter: open, attentive, receptive, engaged, actively involved in the interaction, tangible, embodied. We all need presence to enter into real contact with others.

In this respect, I think the name 'society of screens' is appropriate for the world we live in. Our screens can be windows which open digitally onto infinity, mirrors in which we can contemplate ourselves, but a screen is also a partition which separates us physically from others. Like at the beach: an ideal sun-screen would block out *all* the rays of the sun. 'Just go look at my webpage.' At the moment, I cannot go beyond the screen to touch any real person on the other side, like *Alice in Wonderland* does in the mirror. One day, perhaps, not now. And I can digitize, encode, virtualize anything I want, but none of that will replace the breath of the person I love on my shoulder. That is what we call presence. And the more screens there are, the more we need presence.

We need to touch the Other – be physically close to them, be touched by them. This kind of presence is all the more crucial in times of pandemic, confinement, and lock-down. That is, in situations in which, in a pernicious fashion, the Other tends to come to signify contamination and collective contagion, and in which everyone is required to withdraw and live in isolation. Social distance may then mutate into mental alienation. In circumstances like that, reaffirming the need for speech between people physically present to each other and its role as a bond between humans is a matter of our very survival.

## *'Connectivity' in place of a real bond*

Speech is founded on listening, paying attention, and presence. As such, it can hope to escape being completely swallowed up in the universal maelstrom of electronic noise. There is also some hope that it can escape our contemporary curse, that glimpse into the abyss: *vox clamans in interneto*. There are billions of voices calling out in vain in this desert, all those lost voices that eventually fade away and fall silent for want of anyone listening. Or they are drowned in the chaos or lost in the bustling interstellar confusion of the virtual world; or in the sea of social networks and electronic media. The internet is stuffed so full of buzzes, noises, random images, fragments of text, and so forth, that it has effectively – if paradoxically – become a new kind of desert. It is a diabolical landscape of desolate over-plenitude where all that exists is, on the one hand, shrieking excess and, on the other, unfathomable emptiness, each the mirror image of the other.

To shout loudly is not to speak to someone, and to be 'connected' is not to have a real bond with them. Speaking to each other in the full sense of the term is a way of establishing a bond. Only when someone is listening does speech get its resonance, and only through speech is a bond established. Connectivity alone is not enough; one needs in addition to endow it with a sense, a purpose, a finality. What one really needs in the case in question is a society-based process of re-establishing proper links, interpersonal relations between people. One might say we need to re-initiate a process of 're-liance', both in its original etymological sense (*re* + *lier* = 'bind back' in Old French) and in its current everyday sense of dependence. If I rely on you, I trust you, have confidence in you, and think I can count on you to support me. This is the sense in which I propose that speech must be 'reliable' and which thereby creates bonds between us. When we speak in a 'reliable' way, we are, each of us, bound to ourselves, to the world, and to others. Only this process can give to our actions and our life a sense of what is essential. Speech in the sense intended here should have as its goal bringing us together, rather than dividing us. Allowing us to get past the logorrhoea that forces us ever further down a one-way street toward a world of mutual indifference, failed meetings of minds, and juxtaposed solitudes.

So speech, if it is correctly oriented toward the Other and if all its implications are fully embraced, can create bonds between us. This must be seen as very different from being connected to the network, being, as they say, 'hooked up'. The very use of this latter term expresses the palpable mechanization of humanity which we oppose. A human being is not a machine for producing clicks on a keyboard. Speech allows humanity to unfold, because it creates bonds. It is what allows us to enter into a process in which we domesticate each other, for this is what 'to establish ties' also means, according to the apt account Saint-Exupéry gave in *The Little Prince*.[8]

## Media-induced ultra-soltitude

By creating bonds, speech helps us to struggle against atomization, anomie, pathological detachment, general isolation, extreme individualism, radical intolerance. That is, against a world in which each person sits alone in their own room and every person is (only) for themselves. This isolation has the perverse effect of creating false communities, closed groups, secret conventicles, and radical cells, where the commons imprisons itself, and turns itself into a vain, but recurrent, obsessive illusion. Where each individual turns round and round in their own bubble, withdrawn into their own bunker, locked down in their own silo, caught in the hostile light that shines on them from their computer screen. Each one of us is force-fed the identical stories so that in the end we come to see anyone who is different, in principle anyone other than ourselves, as at best a ridiculous clown, in most cases a radical stranger, and in the worst case a deadly enemy.

You are not like me, hence you are a danger to me. You do not think in the way I do, so I shall not talk to you. You express a point of view different from my own, so you do not exist. *Because I love only myself.* This is narcissism 2.0, the fanaticism which will accept only complete identity, the Other who is a mirror for my complete fixation on myself. Media-induced ultra-solitude – the radical loneliness paradoxically generated by hyperconnectivity. Connectivity, the ability to communicate with others at a distance, has some undeniable advantages. *It is wonderful to be able to see you, my love, at the other end of the earth.* On the other hand, people have never felt as alone as they do now when everyone is completely connected. Edgar Allen Poe's 'man of the crowd' refused to be alone, so he 'stalked backward and forward, without apparent object, among the throng' in the streets.[9] Our state is worse than that envisaged by Baudelaire, in which each person remains 'alone in the middle of a busy crowd', so that 'multitude' and 'solitude' become 'equal and interconvertible terms'.[10] The absence of genuine human contact from which we suffer produces a state of febrile psychic dispersion which is the exact opposite of that other kind of solitude: the fruitful solitude of individual reading. Reading allows us to collect our thought and collect ourselves. It is at one and the same time a mode of immersion in the self, a way of traversing whole new worlds, and a means to enriching one's being. The solitude that surrounds it is one of fullness, not of deficiency. The need for an audience in our world is aggravated by the cult of the self and the obscuring of the Other, and it generates anxiety and depression: *how many likes? Is that all? How much do people love me? That little?*

We are forced back into ourselves, and we wander about the world, unaware, but haunted by our own desire to be recognized. In such a situation, how could we ever encounter the Other, except as an object of prejudice, a projection, something which we reject and of which we disapprove? All of these are distorting lenses which undermine the possibility of establishing a healthy relationship with the Other. 'That which is like me is good; that which differs from me is bad.' This is the morality of those weak in spirit, those with occluded hearts, those who have barricaded themselves off from the world, or of serial trolls. Sometimes the enemies are merely those whose stories we have not heard.

## To have the courage to speak

We need to have the courage to encounter the Other – the courage to accept difference, diversity, complexity, and singularity. The courage to speak (and listen) in a just, sensible, and responsible way. 'Speech' in this sense is something which really does require not just initiative, but also courage, because it requires us to leave our ego-centred comfort zone and move out toward the Other. In other words, we must learn to realign ourselves and overcome what we now are. That is, obviously, a frightening prospect. Taking leave of one's well-established opinions, the entrenched camp into which we can always withdraw, in order to expose oneself – to say who one is, express oneself in public, and submit to the judgement of others; of course that is unsettling. What we risk in this world of pitiless universal censoriousness is, in the worst case scenario, ridicule, humiliation, visible failure, mental breakdown, symbolic degradation, social death.

Three-quarters of us suffer from glossophobia, fear of speaking in public.[11] *Glossophobia* means, literally, fear of the tongue, fear of *live* speech. Fear of whatever is *live*. It is, however, noteworthy that for the most part, those who are terrified of 'speaking in public' are exactly the same people who express themselves in a completely uncontrolled way in the new electronic media, spilling out their opinions so copiously that they flood social networks and the internet – from

WhatsApp groups to individual emails. One runs more risk *live* in person than at a distance.

We need not only to dare to take the floor and speak, but we must also learn how to *hold to what we say*, to keep our word. We must make sure what we say is well founded, but we must then live what we have said, give it substance, carry the burdens associated with it, give an account of it, and accept responsibility for it. The good news is that one can learn to do this.

# Part II

# For a humanism of speech

# 4

# Standing by our words

## Restoring the full meaning of speech

### *Humanity at all levels*

We start with a striking fact. Speech and related terms such as 'talk', 'saying', and 'word(s)' have a very wide range of semantically correct uses: they are expressive of our humanity at all levels and in all dimensions.

Speech signifies, first of all, a special *capacity*, the ability to formulate and express thought in words (as in 'to be human' is to be 'an entity capable of speech'). It also designates the *exercise* of that capacity (as in 'freedom of speech'), the *act* of speaking and its result (as in 'to give a speech'), and finally the *way of speaking* (as in 'her speech was fluent and eloquent'). To be eloquent is to be a master of the power of speech.

'Speech' can designate a sequence of words, but one should note that, even if it is used in this apparently unitary sense, it can have contradictory connotations. On the one hand, it can refer to what is meant by that sequence (the substantial semantic content which is asserted), as in 'his speech summed up what they all believed', but, on the other hand, it can be used in a denigrating way, as in 'That is just speech,' or, more colloquially 'That's just talk.' That means it is empty, mere air, not serious, as opposed to something that is factual, binding, or engraved in stone. 'To keep one's *word*' is to honour a verbal agreement one has made. 'The words' can refer to something well known that was either spoken or written down: 'the words of Zhou Enlai about the French Revolution' or 'the words of Rimbaud'. For Protestants, of course, there is also the special religious usage of 'word', as in 'The Word of God'.

'Speech', 'talk', and 'words' map out the whole range of our humanity, from our most basic cognitive capacities to our forms of action, from our ability to find the right creative word to our penchant for empty chatter. Speech in a sense defines what is there in front of it; it spreads out the domain of all those things which are possible. It opens up the space in which under an infinity of different forms we can express ourselves in our own singular way. The shape we have as people derives from the shape we give speech – and vice versa. I am what I say – and, *ex negativo*, what I do *not* say. Silence can be the most perfect form of eloquence. Even if it does not coincide with what I do, what I say must at any rate reveal what I think, what I feel, what I am pursuing, what I intend to do. Unless, that is, speech is evasive, distorting, manipulative, or perverse and is not merely no good guide to what I will do, but actually hides what I think. Even in that case, however, speech reveals something about me, although that is something completely different from the manifest content of what I say.

## Transparency and the mask

What use, then, do we make of speech? We speak to say *what* exactly? The two extremes here are to say everything or to say nothing. To say everything is the fanatical demand of Alceste, Molière's misanthrope, that champion of Truth, who, as a self-declared absolute man of his word, despises '*ces obligeants diseurs d'inutiles paroles* [ingratiating fellows who spout useless words]':

> *Je veux qu'on soit sincère et qu'en homme d'honneur*
> *On ne lâche un seul mot qui ne parte du cœur*

[I want everyone to be sincere, and, as befits honourable people,/ That no one utters a single word that does not come from the heart][1]

To say nothing is the Machiavellian position people attributed to Talleyrand, the master politician who swore thirteen different oaths of allegiance and served as minister, successively, one after the other, in completely opposed regimes: the Ancien Régime, the Revolution, the Empire, the Restoration, the July Monarchy. Talleyrand is alleged to have said: 'Speech is given to man so that he can disguise what he thinks.'[2] This, of course, is a diplomat's humorous inversion of Molière's 'Speech was given to man so that he could explain what he thinks.'[3] It is not without a certain irony that Molière puts this defence of transparency in the mouth of a character who has the gift of the gab and is using it to try to defraud and despoil his audience, an intolerable logorrheic doctor with the ridiculous, but significant, name 'No-holds-barred-all-round-fighter' (Pancrace). Pancrace, however, as the stage direction informs us, is the kind of person who starts speaking 'at the same time as Sganarelle, without listening to him'. A real champion of listening, then.

On the one side, then, there is the perfect correspondence between speech and reality: I am what I say, and say what I am. This is the fatal flaw of Othello, his naïveté. He has no distance from his own words and ascribes that same candour to others, blind even to the machinations of his worst enemy. On the other side, we find a complete opposition between words and intention. 'I am not what I am.'[4] This is the expression of Iago's murderous treachery, who, passing himself off as a loyal confidant, plays with words and pours into Othello's ears poisonous falsehoods sweetened to sound like vital truths.

This shows the confrontation of these two radical positions – I would say, two different ways in which it is strictly impossible for humans to live together in harmony. On the one hand, total sincerity, with no filters: proclaim out loud everything that comes into your head, pour your heart out completely, say whatever your 'gut' tells you to say. As long as you speak 'your truth', let the consequences be damned. And, on the other hand, perpetual duplicity, calculated dissimulation: say nothing of what you think; as long as you are able to advance your interests, to hell with being 'true to yourself'. One problem that remains is that my glances may betray what I think; they may 'speak' despite my best efforts of concealment:

> *Vous n'aurez point pour moi de langages secrets:*
> *J'entendrai des regards que vous croirez muets*
>
> [You will have no language that is secret from me/ I'll understand the glances which you think give nothing away][5]

This is the cruel language Nero uses in Racine's *Britannicus* when he threatens to kill Julia's lover unless she herself rebuffs him, before hiding to observe their rendezvous. Speech is a matter of just measure, but also something that can be mastered.

### Leaving infancy behind. Speaking as overcoming

That means speech is something that must be learned, something one needs to work at, think about and think with, learn to shape, learn to use expressively. Speech develops, mutates, and is passed on from one person to another as we elaborate it, and it, in turn, has a transformative effect on those who use it. Speech implies commitment. Having the capacity to speak, and to stick to your word, makes you a person. It is no accident that 'word' means both a solemn promise ('I give you my word') and the most trivial thing one can imagine ('Words, words, words'). It all depends on the context and what you make of it. What is certain is that we need to appreciate in what way and to what extent speech is the foundation of our existence. To what extent words constitute us as the beings we are, and to what extent thought itself comes about only in and through words. As Wittgenstein puts it: 'What we cannot speak about we must pass over in silence.'[6] What we are able to express to some extent determines what we can think, as Boileau writes:

*Ce que l'on conçoit bien s'énonce clairement*
*Et les mots pour le dire arrivent aisément*

[What is well thought out is easy to formulate,/ And the words to say it are easy to find][7]

Finally, our mode of expression gives form to what we wish to say. Victor Hugo saw this clearly when he explained that the form of something that was said was its foundation, which, however, had risen to the surface.[8] Speech is an adventure which constitutes the foundation of our humanity, the network of girders that supports our being in the world; we need to take care of it. It must be worked over until it is in good shape. We need to cultivate speech until we have mastered it.

The *infans*,[9] etymologically, is a human who does not speak – does not *yet* speak – the young child in the first stage of life, who does not yet know what it is to speak, doesn't grasp the point of speech. As such, they are not fully conscious of language, fully aware of the responsibilities associated with speaking, or fully in control of their own speech.

That, in a way, is the situation in which we find ourselves today. We have relapsed into a state that is not exactly infantile in the worst sense, but it is immature: a state in which we are at the mercy of momentary impulses, unable to tolerate frustration, impatient with others, and in which we act inconsistently, and fall prey to unpredictable bouts of extreme anger. We desperately need to put this behind us and grow up. It is a sign of immaturity to need always to *oppose* something, or to shout and scream at the top of one's lungs, in order to take a position at all. Becoming an adult means learning to control oneself. Adolescence is the age of feeling universally put upon, pouting, having crying fits, falling to rages about trivialities, and scapegoating. This is what we need to overcome in ourselves. Not everything that comes out of the mouths of babes is the pristine truth. Because the child lacks self-restraint, impulse control, and a sense of limits and moderation, bold-faced lies, monstrous cruelty, unbridled rage, and limitless violence can also emerge. We all need to learn how to keep our impulses in check and focus them if we wish to live together with others. We need to be able to detach ourselves from our existing opinions and commitments and potentially get beyond them if we wish to live in harmony with one another. We need to speak to one another rather than murder each other.

### *From language as a mere instrument to fully realized speech*

Since one can make 'speech' mean virtually anything one wishes, it is important here to say in exactly what sense the term is being used. What do I mean by 'speech'? 'Speech' is language in action, words coming to life. It arises from our nature, and is the distinguishing feature of humans. It is something we think can be taken for granted, something too obvious to mention – after all, everyone speaks. It is held up as an aspiration – everyone wants to speak. In fact, it is an art, because not everyone inhabits the world of speech in the same way.

So that we have a clear basis for continuing, I should like to define speech in the following way: it is a special kind of oral performance or a gestural performance using sign language.

In his *Course in General Linguistics*, Saussure distinguishes between three French terms: *langue, langage,* and *parole.*[10]

The first of these designates a specific, conventional system of human communication, distinct from others, such as Chinese, Russian, French, or English; we might say in English that this is 'language' in the sense of a particular 'tongue'. The second refers to language in general as a universal capacity, with which humans are endowed and which permits them to construct particular 'tongues' in order to communicate. 'Language' in this second sense (*langage*) is innate, whereas a particular tongue (*langue*) is acquired. A particular tongue, like English or French, rests on social conventions, which are transmitted and enforced by a group and which pre-exist any given individual. I can't really be said to be speaking 'English' unless a whole set of expectations and conventions is already in place before I start. (Which does not, of course, mean that I cannot through my speaking and writing influence or even change some of those expectations.) The third term in Saussure's triad, *parole*, designates the particular, personal use some given person makes of some existing tongue (*langue*) – the use some individual makes of the universal capacity we have to communicate (*langage*). So *parole* marks out the concrete relation that exists between each individual and a particular tongue (*langue*). It is the result of exchanges with other speakers, which will usually take place in the medium of one or another of the natural languages (*langues*).

Natural languages are gestural and visual forms of expression and they operate by means of signs, or they are oral, using sounds, especially the sound of the human voice.

Oral communication takes place when a message is transmitted by the living voice of a speaker to a group of listeners.

A performance is the realization of an act of speaking in some concrete situation; it is putting speech into real use. So, archetypically, an actor or musician might say 'I performed well last night' or 'It was a good performance.' One can see then that in this sense linguistic 'performance' is completely different from the purely teleological activity which was envisaged when discussing 'eloquence'. In that context, what was at issue was effectiveness in convincing an audience, success. So, on the one hand, 'performance' can mean enacting speech, realizing it, but then, on the other hand, it is sometimes used to mean impact. What we need to do is to embrace speech as performance, while not reducing it to the dimension of eloquence alone with its exclusive focus on producing a particular effect on an audience.

## Restoring the full potency of speech

### Speech at the heart of all human activities

I wish to discuss nine essential dimensions or modalities of speech, each with its own characteristic form and dynamic:

- Speech as an *ability* or capacity, a singular way of actually using language (*langage*).
- Speech as *action*, as a real oral or gestural performance.
- Speech as *revelation*, as a personal way of formulating who one is.
- Speech as *manifestation*, as a way in which one is distinctively marked by the language (*langue*, tongue) one uses.
- Speech as *enunciation*, as the verbalized expression of a thought.
- Speech as *declaration*, as containing a concrete message addressed to an audience.
- Speech as a form of *socialization*, a form of commitment to social interaction and positive engagement with others.
- Speech as *narrative*, as a way in which a living voice passes down stories.
- Speech as *creation*, as an original verbal act.

It is because all of these dynamic features of speech are in play that I can say to myself: 'I am speaking. Something speaks to me. We speak to each other.'

## *The power of the good. Speech and its essential properties*

So, clearly, I use 'speech' in a very emphatic sense, in the strongest sense in which it is possible to take the term. 'Speech' is to be contrasted with the 'message' which is being transmitted in what I say (for instance, that you should now leave the building); also with the 'proposition' which is being enunciated (for instance, 'This building is on fire'); and finally with what is sometimes called 'discourse', in that 'discourse' designates a complex discursive exposition of some topic which has a particular slant or orientation. 'Speech' in this strong sense is in fact distinct from all the other specific phenomena mentioned in my account up to now by virtue of the specific properties it has: it is embodied, it is, among other things, a form of listening and of addressing an audience, it has meaning, it is interactive, it is associated with responsibilities, and it must be appropriate to the circumstances.

There are forms of speech which are only apparently valuable and worthy: advertising, for instance. There are pseudo-forms of speech – the mere transmission of messages. And there are duplicitous forms of speech: propaganda. There is violent speech, angry speech, destructive speech. Not all speech is sweetness and light, benevolence and truth, peace and goodwill on earth. Far from it. No one can fail to notice this. Nevertheless, if one takes 'speech' in its fullest and most substantial sense, it at least has the merit of encompassing systematically all the dimensions of human existence. If we were able to unfold and cultivate speech fully, human life would not confront us in a completely raw, disordered state, but would at the very least have been filtered and conceptually integrated. If we are concerned with the full cultivation of our humanity, we need to be sure that all the relevant dimensions have been taken into consideration. Speech should be structured with a view to bringing out its principal goal: the realization of humanity in all its forms and all respects. The structure we give it is a construct, but one that provides human life with a logic and a meaning. In a certain sense, this is an instance of a kind of formalization, because one is attributing to life an aesthetics, a form; also a kind of expressivity – a poetics, a style. Taking account of the Other is a part of the construct, so it can also be said to contain an ethics, and an orientation toward a kind of justice. Finally, because of the global and unitary nature of the structure which speech exhibits, the focus on speech will be associated with a certain kind of politics, one which puts the emphasis on balance between the various elements in the construct.

When, then, in what follows, I use the term 'speech', I mean speech in this very strong sense. I don't mean offensive, aggressive rantings, or manipulative verbal interventions – propaganda – but reasonable, responsible, appropriate speech. I mean speaking with honesty and commitment, acting in the realm of words in a way that makes them a living expression of our full, essential humanity. Speech should be a realm in which conscientious engagement and real encounters between diverse people take place, where the Other can feel at home and meaning can emerge. This kind of speech will have to be holistic and pay attention to all aspects of the situation. It will be a medium in which my relation to myself, my relation to the Other, and my relation to the world all find their proper active equilibrium.

Given the present degraded state of 'communication', it is urgent that we create the conditions for such a form of speech to exist, a form of speech worthy of the name: valuable, worthwhile speech oriented toward collective human well-being. Note that speech in this sense is not the same thing as what is sometimes called 'speaking well' (producing rhetorically well-turned phrases) and even less is it something like evangelical proselytizing ('preaching the good word' in the etymological sense: *evangelium* = good word).[11] We are not a bunch of naïve idealists, Pollyannas, babes-in-arms, or visionary flower people. Rather, we are the representatives of a humanism which our digital epoch desperately needs. Our commitment is to living speech and complex thought in the era of *Thumbelina* and of 'click-and-connect'.[12] In our situation, our goal must be to find an appropriate form of speech which enunciates and promotes justice, the conscientious pursuit of meaning, reasonableness, and intelligence, and which fosters the creation and cultivation of ties and relations between people. In short, a form of speech that fosters and develops our humanity.

### *Humanity in action. Speech in all its dimensions*

This text is an appeal to all its readers to elaborate and deploy 'speech' in all of its dimensions: anthropological, philosophical, aesthetic, poetic, ethical, and political.

*In the anthropological dimension*, speech is to be construed as the foundation of our humanity, as an art of making sense, giving shape to ideas, and reassigning to words their appropriate weight, substance, and significance. Speech is a way in which we are fully present to each other. We need to give spoken words their anchorage in reality, their life context, their full embodied consistency; this is even more important in our era of de-materialization than it was before. Speech is the art of interaction, and its role should be to help bring about real changes in which all those involved fully understand what is at stake.

*In the aesthetic dimension*, we must treat speech as an act of creation, as the art which can evoke things, as a poetic power, a form of expressive vitality. This is the dimension of symbolic elaboration, of placing reality in a wider perspective provided by the imagination. It is also the place for an art of interpretation, the unfolding of possible meanings which opens us up to an infinity of plural worlds. Speech in the proper sense is characterized by a fruitful kind of polysemy, and has an irreducible complexity; what is said does not, in general, have a single simple meaning. True speech represents the opposite extreme of narrow literal-mindedness, the banal transmission of platitudes in the guise of information, and the unambiguous certitude that kills the spirit. Speech is the art of the present – in specific concrete acts, it crystallizes a particular moment – and also the art of immediate experience, because in it living subjects reveal themselves in an original way which expresses their whole personality.

*In the ethical dimension*, speech is internally linked with *moral responsibility*. In order to listen in the way which speech demands, we must make an effort to exercise our powers of paying attention to others and of being open to what they say. This requires us to concentrate and to have the courage to exercise the virtue of hospitality: we must learn to control ourselves, take a step back from our own desires and projects, and recognize and accept that which is different. If speech is taken, as it properly should be, as the art of addressing the Other, that means that it should inculcate in us a sensitivity to those being spoken to – those 'others' who must in every respect be my concern. As an art which makes us both more aware of what we are doing and more conscious of its ethical implications, speech is the basis for authentic encounters between people. Finally, as an art of dialogue, the cultivation of proper speech should lead to mutual respect, reciprocity in our relations with others, and even the preservation of the conditions under which alone dialogue is possible.

*In the political dimension*, speech has a *collective dynamic* of its own which must be protected and allowed to flourish. It is the art of changing how we think and sharing our conceptions – and we must learn to share even those which we do not ourselves embrace. By speaking, we act in the world and thereby transform reality itself. Speech is the art of commitment, of changing one's given position and going beyond oneself for the sake of a cause. One aspect of this is the ability to bring people together on the basis of what they share, despite acknowledging their differences. This means joining together scattered forces and assembling them in the same place, so that in debate one can deal with opposing points of view. But speech also requires an ability to express violence without completely denying it in order to focus and channel it, and the ability to formulate tensions, bring out points of disagreement, and expose conflicts in order the better to be able to transcend them. The common narrative which our shattered society needs can be provided only by a form of speech which can articulate what connects us – more than that which divides us – can open gates, create lasting bonds, build bridges where walls are being erected, and, eventually, bring peace to the city and reconciliation to society.

It is in this sense that we have a responsibility to come together to allow speech to live, flourish, and expand. The way to do this is by elevating it.

# 5

# Elevating speech

## Restoring the dignity of the spoken word

### Keeping your word

'Elevating speech' means, in the first instance, detaching it from its present degraded state and giving it back its dignity. One can start this process by insisting that people keep their word, which means that they live in conformity with their speech, remaining fully in accord with what they say – both at any given moment and over the course of time. People need to feel that they are bound by what they say. This is the only way in which words can, once again, count for something. My word is my bond. What I say today will hold tomorrow, too. And what I say has the same standing as my written promise; it has the same truth value and is equally reliable. That is the case, of course, within my given framework of reference and relative to what I know, and so I need humility, a lucid sense of my own limits, and an ability to be self-critical to protect myself from asserting more than I can warrant.

In short, keeping your word, sticking to what you say, means treating our speech as if it was something that could constrain us – it sticks to us as much as we should stick to it. 'A man doesn't let himself do that kind of thing,' as Camus puts it,[1] adding that this phrase which his father used was the only thing that remained of him, who died in the First World War when Camus was just one year old. This is what it means to receive responsibility as a legacy. Human beings can restrain themselves, exercise self-control, pull themselves back from acting, and also go beyond themselves – they can stand up straight and hold to their commitments. The framework that makes this possible – the set of bones and muscles that lets us stand and remain standing upright – is, to a large extent, speech. It is what guarantees sense, and gives us a reliable foundation for acting; it is what underwrites all our certainties and all the promises we make to others. Whatever stable self-confidence we have we find in speech because it gives us the power of adjusting to the world, expressing ourselves appropriately, and thinking, acting, and talking with moderation. It is speech which allows me to acquire consistency of purpose and action by binding and holding me together in time, attaching me to the path which I pursue through life, and creating the sediment which constitutes to a large degree my coherent substance, as the person I am. Speech is what allows us to stand upright and face up to ourselves and others by making it possible for us to overcome and go beyond what we happen to be, by providing a firm foundation for our interactions, by fostering exchanges with others, and by creating a dynamic in which both parties improve themselves and their relationship.

Entities who are endowed with the power of speech and who keep their word cause us to respect them – and rightly so. Their dignity, integrity, and rectitude speak for themselves. The respect they show for their own given word; their *noblesse oblige*: their faithfulness to their commitments, to their values and ideals; their persistence in being true to themselves and to others; their ability to step aside from their own narrow self-interest and point of view and pass beyond it to accept the transcendence of the Other – whether that Other be a divine being, or simply my neighbours, as creatures with a human face: all these are the virtues *par excellence* of chivalry, of the medieval knight as an archetype of nobility of character. One can sum this disposition up in a single word: loyalty. Or, to invoke even more strongly the historical origins of this virtue, one can use the original Latin term: *fides*. This word means 'trust', 'confidence', 'faith', 'creditworthiness'; then 'sincerity', 'authenticity', 'promise', 'fidelity', 'trustworthiness', 'reliable assistance'. *Fides*, then, is the keystone of all relationships; it is the condition under which alone a 'lasting agreement' (*foedus*) can be achieved with the Other. *Fides/foedus* are words derived from the same root, and they provide the same reliable foundation for action. For society to exist, people must keep faith with each other; stand by their word. They must affirm themselves by showing themselves to be creatures of their word, beings whose word can be *trusted*. This quality is not a superannuated relic of the feudal nobility of ages long past, but a property of all honourable people. The negative counterpart of the person of honour is the traitor, the perjuror, the criminal, the person who is forsworn. The person who does not adhere to what they say, and who thereby destroys the confidence which people must have in the given word, betrays the tacit social pact on which all relations are built, and undermines the foundations on which society rests. Such a person is a villain, 'subtle, false, and treacherous', as that worst of kings and enemy of the human race, Shakespeare's Richard III, openly declares himself to be.[2]

In this age of hyperbolic suspicion, it is important to re-establish trust. We must find a way to trust in ourselves again, and in the Other. Trust what we are told; have trust in humanity. What is relevant here is not merely what I *say* (strictly speaking), but also what I really mean; what goal I am pursuing; where I'm tending; what underlies and forms the background of my words; my real intention and the firmness of purpose I exhibit over time. When I speak, it is not just a matter of accidentally letting something slip – I must adhere to my word, just as my word binds me; what I say commits me in the present and over time. My words must be the activation of who I am, they must make the story of my life consistent, and they must give a direction to my development. All of this is revealed by the way I keep my word. This is true whether I am speaking explicitly in words or in signs, because the language of signs and gestures can be just as eloquent as that of sounds or marks on paper. Sign language is also a form of language. Here, too, what is important is how my speech binds me and how it creates connections and bonds with others.

## To move from ego to lego

For people to speak to each other in the strong sense is for them to create links and relations between themselves in the real world. It is to leave the domain of unilateral broadcasting of one's own opinions and to enter into an authentic relationship; to extract oneself from tit-for-tat polemics and commit oneself to forms of speech that create bonds between people. We need to overcome the tendency to ask 'What's in it for me?' and learn to see the larger scheme of things and identify with its interests. People must be encouraged to crawl out of their self-imposed solitary confinement and become part of a social constellation. This is what I mean by moving from ego to *lego*.

*Lego*: this word has multiple senses and its derivatives appear in a variety of different languages, with slightly different connotations. Etymology, however, permits us to grasp the original meaning, from which the multitude of further senses develop. *Lego* comes from the Indo-European root *\*leǵ-* meaning 'collect, assemble, put together'. It thus designates the essence of what I mean by speech: speech is linkage, connection. In ancient Greek, the original sense of *lego* is still present. Λέγω can still be used to mean 'put together': choose, select, pick out. In addition, there are a number of slightly different secondary meanings: to assert, to tell someone something, to speak in a way that makes sense, to mean, to designate, to signify; also, to narrate, read aloud, sing, address an audience like an orator. In the Latin word *lĕgō*, the first meaning of the root is the dominant one of collect, choose, and pick, and versions of the second appear only in specific contexts: *lĕgō* as 'assembling with one's eyes or ears, passing something in review, reading, reading aloud'. This last usage gives rise to the French verb *lire* and the Italian *leggere*, both meaning straight-forwardly 'to read'. Finally, the Danish word *lege* means 'to play', from which is derived LEGO, those plastic blocks which, as everyone knows, can be put together by children to build things. They get their name from the Danish expression *leg godt* ('play well').[3]

Λέγω, *lĕgō*, LEGO. They designate different ways of putting things together. Now put together these three descendants of the Indo-European *\*lĕǵ*, the Greek, the Latin, and the Danish, and if you integrate them correctly, what you will get is an account of what holds us all together as humans: our ability to select, choose, run through, speak, speak in a sensible way (signify, intend), speak artfully (recite, narrate, sing, address like an orator), collect and discriminate (with eyes and ears), read, read out loud, play, represent. So these three derivatives of *lego* unify in themselves nine fundamental qualities of speech: the ability to make linkages, to discriminate, run through and hold together what we see or hear, to mean, to address an audience with eloquence, to read, to play/pretend/ represent, to assemble diverse things, to construct. Or, one might say, to make connections, and discern distinctions, to imagine and mean. To formulate and summarize. To read and understand. To interpret and to speak well. To put together and build up. To act reasonably and to make all our actions (in some sense) works of art.

This is what speech aspires to at its best: to be a medium through which people are connected, and to be itself a link between them. Speech in this sense is a synonym of 'intelligence', that human capacity which, by an extraordinary coincidence, originally means 'ability to connect that which is disparate' (*interlego*). So one more instance of a derivative of *\*leǵ* and one that adds a number of further semantic connotations to the mix, because now different notions of '*inter*' (*inter*- connections) become relevant. This verbal connection between *lego* and *intelligence* is not a matter of historical accident, but a result of the fact that the two share, in principle, a common vocation: *lego* is, by its very essence, the heart of intelligence. Intelligence is the art of seeing and creating connections; speech is intelligence in action.

## Promoting right speech

### Four forms of rightness

After these preliminaries, we can now treat the conditions under which speech is right.

I distinguish four forms of rightness: right with regard to oneself; right toward others; right in its principles; right in action. Corresponding to each of these, there is a major issue that arises. These four issues are: questions about my own control over and mastery of speech; questions about the linkage which is created by speech; questions of meaning; and finally questions about the way in which the rightness of speech is concretely realized. First, I am myself the only judge of whether I have mastered speech, that is, whether my speech is right with regard to myself, true to me and who I am. Second, however, the nature of the link I create to others in speaking is always in principle an open question. Third, what is right in principle is the question of the meaning of what I do. Finally, rightness is concretely realized by being manifested in action.

There are two distinct modalities of speech: one can think of speech as having the right relation to something or as being inherently an action of the right kind. The four forms of rightness are further specifications of these: speech as having a right *relation* to self or to the Other, speech as right action, in the sense that the action is right either in principle or in practice. These various distinctions also cut across each other in systematically changing ways. When it comes to discussing the origin of speech, are we interested in the concrete subject who speaks or in the (potentially abstract) thought expressed in speech? If, however, we are interested in the goal of speech, the question is whether it is to be construed essentially as directed to the Other or as having as its end its own realization in an act.

## *The conditions of right speech*

Here, then, is my list of the conditions for right speech:

I.  Speech must be essential; it must be the foundation of everything.
    1. Speech is the foundation of humanity.
II. Speech must be right with regard to myself; it must be something I have in my control.
    2. Speech mobilizes *the whole of my being*: body, heart, spirit; reason, the imagination, the will, the senses; my emotions, my sentiments, my passions, my impulses, my sensations, my thoughts, my processes of reasoning.
    3. Speech *commits one to responsibility* – here one must consider issues of freedom, autonomy, dignity, subjectivity, singularity.
    4. Speech presupposes *authenticity* – and thus raises issues of candour, sincerity, fair dealing, honesty, good faith, loyalty.
    5. Speech requires *control* – so it involves questions of self-mastery, moderation, steadiness of purpose, composure, self-restraint.

6. Speech operates by *alignment* – and so there arise questions of agreement, consistence, coherence, congruence.

7. Speaking demands *courage* – speakers must be resolute, have confidence, self-assurance, resilience, perseverance, force of character, and they must be able to go beyond their own boundaries and act outside their comfort zone.

III. Speaking must be right in relation to the Other. It must be a form of connection.

8. Speech presupposes *the Other* – this is the realm of ethics and issues about open-mindedness, benevolence, tolerance, respect, considerateness, recognition.

9. Speech requires that people *listen* – so here we need to address matters of attention, focus, empathy, comprehension.

10. *Orientation toward an audience* is an integral part of speech – so who is being addressed? To what end? What expectations do speakers and hearers have? How is speech received? What reaction does it call forth?

11. Speech requires an *exchange* between people. Is there a proper dialogue? What about issues of reciprocity, the sharing of resources, information, and power? What about balance? Do both parties get to speak in turn? Are opposing views represented?

12. Speech establishes firm *links* between people – here there arise issues about rapprochement, close conjunction, interaction, encounters between people, *reliance*, linkage.

13. Speech tends to lead to *bringing people together into groups* – so here we find questions about mutual comprehension, conciliation, peace-making, reconciliation, association, federation, reconnection.

IV.  Speech must be right in principle. It must be reasoned.

14.  Speech provides an active focus for *consciousness* – it involves and stimulates thought, intelligence, discernment, the spirit of criticism, lucidity, careful examination.

15.  Speech must have a *meaning* – express an idea, be about something, have an intention, a signification, a direction, an aim.

16.  To speak is to make a tacit appeal for *relevant precision* – for staying on the topic, articulating the given situation clearly and exactly, for sharpness of perception and argumentation, nuance, sophistication, subtlety, for an appreciation of complexity.

17.  Speech authorizes *interpretation* – we can always give a 'reading' of what is said, a commentary on it, an exegesis; we can look for analogies, transpose ideas, motifs, and expressions; we can give variations on what is said; speech is polysemous and plurivocal.

18.  To speak means to accept *discussion*, the give-and-take of question and answers, the response to what is said, the rebuttal, the counterclaim, divergence of opinions, disagreement, the formulation of objections, the contesting of claims, contradiction, controversy.

19.  Speech tolerates *criticism*, analysis, examination, investigation, verification, correction of errors, refutation, attacks on the speaker's attitude, intentions, or behaviour, judgement.

20.  Speech encourages *taking a step back* from things – humour, irony, the bon mot, jokes, banter, satire, play with incongruity, parody, caricature, subversion.

V.  Speech must be right as the action that it is, that is, it must be realized – actually incarnated – in the world.

21.  Speech needs *presence* to be real – so there arise issues about the body, the way speech is anchored in the world, the forms of engagement with which it is asso-

ciated, the particular modalities of its production and reception, questions of contact between speaker and audience.

22. Speech needs *to take its time* – so speakers and audience must have at their disposal time, but also space, patience, and continuing attention; moments have to be reserved for speech to deploy itself and develop.

23. Speech demands *strenuous work* on the part of speakers and listeners – it is an activity that requires focus, investment of time and energy, concentration, effort.

24. Speech requires *elaboration* – it needs to be processed, vetted, edited, to have its logic revealed more clearly; it needs to be composed and constructed, given a form, and turned into a finished work.

25. Speech expresses itself in a particular *form* – in a language which has a poetics, an aesthetics, a style, a register; it belongs to a particular genre; it has a tone, a texture, a structure, a wording; it uses particular turns of phrase.

26. Speech realizes itself in *performance* – only when it is enacted is it truly itself, so here we find questions about speech as a living activity which potentially has real effects.

27. Speech has whatever value it has because of its resonance – the background that sets it off is silence.

In my view, these are the conditions for rightness of speech, the conditions under which speech is good, beneficial, benevolent, fruitful, productive, constructive, and harmonious.

How can we bring such speech into existence and make it a concrete reality? Through a philosophy and an ethics of speech. That is the case theoretically. Practically, we do this by cultivating speech as the art of arts.

# Part III

# Humanity lost, humanity regained

# Speech elevated

# 6

# The seven arts of speech: Cultivating our humanity

## A new approach.
## The arts of speech in the strong sense

### *Special forces of excellence*

To enhance speech and re-establish it in its proper state, we need to raise it to the status of an art. This is the only way to pull it out of the current state of degradation into which it has totally collapsed. Only by mobilizing and deploying a coalition of the best powers available to us can we resurrect it. We need to concentrate all our available resources and powers to put speech back on its feet again and restore it to the status it deserves. We need an elite group of special forces, specifically chosen for the purpose of reversing the current trends we described at the beginning of this essay. And we need to use this group as a commando force with a mission: to allow speech to realize its essence and give it back its proper dignity, status, value, and power. Speech has been counted out, but it can recover its crown and turn defeat into victory.

In other words, in order once again to be able to deploy speech in the strong sense – particularly in this hour of its apparent humiliation – we need to convoke all the forces of

creativity at our disposal. These are paradoxically dependent
on speech, but at the same time they are the foundations on
which it rests. We need to reunite those arts which from the
dawn of time have allowed us again and again to reinvent and
cultivate speech, to shape and develop it, to cherish and value
it. These arts promote speech and they encourage it on the
path toward realizing its own true essence. They are its bread
and butter, and also its patent of nobility; by embodying it at
its very best they raise speech to a higher level, give it life and
make it worthy of honour; they transfigure, exalt, and magnify
it. In short, to save speech we need to call the arts of speech to
our aid, provided that we can infuse them with new inspira-
tional power.

## The quintessence of art

Trying to give an 'absolute' definition of 'art', even if that were
to turn out to be possible, would be a completely different
project from the one I am pursuing here. But still the notion of
'art', like that of 'speech', is too crucial to my argument for me
to fail to give some account of what I mean by it, at least for the
purposes of this discussion, even if it is not possible to do that
in a fully comprehensive and absolute way.

Arts are *acquired* competencies, and to that extent they
differ from natural gifts or forms of innate genius. You must
learn them by mastering particular techniques and methods.
An art is constituted by a set of rules that govern know-how
of a certain kind. Arts are located in places where knowing-
how and knowing-that overlap, where theory meets practice
and habitual expertise encounters experience. Arts establish
alchemical connections between reason and the imagination,
the hand and the soul, obedience to the established ways and
creativity, lucidity and illumination, heritage and rupture,
tradition and innovation. They are something different from
mere crafts and also from the mere habitual application of

techniques. Arts need to mobilize a whole battery of conscious procedures in the service of an end in view.

Despite this, works of art arise from and give expression to unconscious motives, idiosyncratic ideas, and utterly unthought-of associations and projections. They are the fruit of a uniquely individual sensibility and a set of conceptions that are highly personal, both conjoined and held together by inspiration born from a radical and novel desire. When all of these factors work together in the right way, art can transcend the established rules and create original works. Art is the place where subject, project, and object meet, where the imaginary and the real are joined. To be able to express this conjunction at the very highest level of vividness and of truth is a complex and delicate task that requires the full collaboration of a number of distinct elements: the artist must have a broad acquaintance with the world and human experience, mastery of technique, talent, skill, diligence, and the ability to integrate different forms of cognition and to find gestures that are convincing. Great art must be given time, time for the artist to experiment with possibilities, and to allow acquired techniques to bed in; time for the artist to travel down the *via dolorosa* of palpable error in the quest for perfection, while continuing to exercise the virtue of humility by starting from scratch again and again and again.

Art sustains and supports the audacity involved in all innovation, the strength needed to engage in original creation, the courage required to produce revolutions, and it is the foundation of those dazzling moments of revelation which are characteristic of the greatest works. The work of art bears the marks of its origin as the realization of a vision, the objectification of an inspiration, a particular way of experiencing and reacting emotionally to the sensible world. One must see a work of art at the same time as the expression of a singular subjectivity and the result of a long process of apprenticeship. In great art, the production of form, the choice of a language, is also the irruption into the world of something completely original. Nevertheless, the work is always the fruit of hard labour. The 'work of the poet' as Philippe Jaccottet puts it, is 'a laborious attempt to see'.[1]

## Those arts which are a vital necessity

This way of looking at art allows us to get beyond the Manichaean distinction between defining the arts by their instrumental functions (their usefulness) or defining them in a completely non-utilitarian (aesthetic) way. It thus constitutes a return to the Greek conception of art as *techné*. *Τέχνη* means first of all handicraft ('art' as in 'arts-&-crafts', industry, skill, the 'art' of the artisan), but then it also can be used to refer to technique (including technical tricks, clever expedients, shortcuts), and also to 'art' in the sense of the ability to produce original works, to such works themselves, or to the ability to deploy certain forms of theoretical knowledge. Construed in this broad sense, as a successor to *τέχνη*, in addition to its aesthetic vocation, art produces works that have value along a number of different dimensions. It does not confine itself to the strictly non-instrumental; the idea that *all* art must be exclusively 'for its own sake' is drummed into us *ad nauseam*, but the point of this insistence on *l'art pour l'art* is that it is a convenient way of disqualifying art as irrelevant to real human life. It is a prelude to going on to claim that art is a complete waste of time and energy, an 'inessential form of economic activity', in a historical period in which only what is useful should count. As we have heard people say again and again, all of Shakespeare is not worth a single pair of sturdy shoes.[2]

We take a completely different view of the matter. The 'arts of speech' are defined here specifically in such a way as to conjoin their orientation toward inherent aesthetic value with concrete social and political usefulness. If one thinks of the vocation of the arts of speech in this way, it is clearly one that is humanly essential. These arts are not merely attempting to produce beauty – this is a widely recognized aim of 'fine art'. Nor are the arts simply ways of creating meaning – a further task which is widely acknowledged as important, but often attributed to our cognitive capacities. Nor do the arts of speech merely share the goal of technology: the discovery and invention of the useful. Rather, these arts share with ethics a commitment to the right and the just, and with political morality a commitment to the common good. The beautiful, the right, the just, the meaningful, the useful, each of these five is an absolutely essential concern of the arts of speech.

## A healthy diversity

I have spoken about 'the arts of speech' in an abstract stipulative way, but what concretely are these 'arts' that I am discussing? I reject the reduction of the 'arts of speech' to eloquence or rhetoric, to the traditional art of speaking well. I therefore very deliberately try always to use the plural, the *arts* of speech. Partly, the reason for this is that, in view of the gravity of our contemporary situation, eloquence alone is not enough. In fact, the cooptation of the 'art of speech' by eloquence is exactly part of our problem: speech in the full sense is reduced to speaking eloquently, and eloquence is just a kind of performance judged solely by its actual persuasive effect. This means that speech is completely subjected to its actual, momentary success in moving people to action.

This is why I insist on the intrinsic diversity of the arts of speech (in my sense of the term) and on the fortunate fact that they are multiple and distinct, substantially autonomous and internally rich. This is why I employ the plural, and this plurality of the arts of speech is an essential part of their characteristic nature. They all have an obvious family resemblance, but it is the singularity of each one, their differences, and the distinct virtues of each which is the most relevant fact about them. They exhibit a healthy complementarity within an over-all commitment to a common end.

## Overlapping of territories as a virtue

It only remains, then, to circumscribe the domain within which the arts of speech act and to specify the particular dis-ciples which are included in the term. The arts of speech can be distinguished from the plastic, visual, and spatial arts by reference to what it is they try to shape aesthetically. The latter are concerned with visual and spatial forms, with volumes, with particular materials, and with images, whereas the former are primordially dependent on words. The arts of speech share with literature the use of language as their medium, but for the arts of speech what is central is the *act* of speaking, that is, oral performance or performance in sign language.

The arts of speech overlap partially with the arts that are concerned with dramatic staging, but the dramatic arts have a more extensive range in that they include forms of perfor-mance that are not essentially accompanied by words, for instance dance, the circus, street arts, magic, puppetry, mime. They also overlap, but to a lesser extent, with those other live or performing arts which add to staging purely instrumental music, with, however, no vocal or verbal component. Finally, they overlap the least with the 'dramatic arts', as these are construed in most university courses, because they include not only theatre, dance, and music, but also cinema.

These distinctions form the beginning of a classification, but they do not constitute anything like a formal definition because, among other reasons, they describe in the first instance what the arts of speech are *not*, rather than what they are.

*A new meaning for 'arts of speech'; their goal is crucial*

Ordinary usage is of no further help here. Generally, when one encounters the term 'arts of speech', it is used to refer to narrative, to the stories people tell about their lives, the testimony of witnesses, oral literature, or to the arts of diction, enunciation, declamation. Or to the arts of the voice, for instance to systematic attempts to attain euphony in speaking. Or to the oral dimension of human behaviour as a whole. Or to all of these different phenomena at once. Sometimes theatre is included, but theatre also exceeds the boundaries of mere speech. The ways in which the term 'the arts of speech' can be used in everyday life are protean and extremely varied. Our use is open-textured and expressive, and we are constantly extending it to encompass the burgeoning new meanings which the concept generates. On the other hand, there is something elusive, fluctuating, unstable, and imprecise about the exact meaning of 'the arts of speech' (in my sense). There is no clear framework and single determinate perspective, and this is why the concept is at best only partially ever given the full semantic weight it deserves. As a consequence, the arts of speech are stifled and rarely realize their full vocation.

I wish, then, to give this expression 'the arts of speech' a new and original sense, and assign to these arts a preeminent value. They are skills which permit us to deploy and perfect speech in the full, strong sense effectively, in all its power. This is what they are really about. Their vocation is the realization and use of speech, in all its dimensions, with all its implications, speech as the quintessence of our humanity. The cultivation of these arts serves to mobilize, discipline, and elaborate speech, and to give it structure. They thereby help us to sublimate, limit, and transcend violence – to put it completely behind us. This is why I consider them so vitally important in this time of dehumanization. This is why I give them a central place in the struggle to overcome our contemporary forms of conflict.

## An organic whole. The seven pillars of speech

*The common vocation. Arts of collective construction*

I recognize seven of these arts of speech, each one chosen because it seems to be well adapted to countering the contemporary degradation of speech. Each one is selected because I think it can be effective against a particular destructive tendency. My proposal is, therefore, a particular response to a concrete situation. Together these disciplines can help us deal with a series of maladies that have debased us, eaten away at our humanity, and ravaged our societies. I wish to put these seven arts together because they are all powerful and immediately relevant attempts to find solutions to the same problem. They are diverse but complementary.

These seven arts give us the power to use speech as a way to reconnect with each other, provided only that we are willing to devote ourselves fully to them and to employ them in the way I propose. This qualification is necessary because, as should be immediately obvious, each of these arts can pass over to the dark side, and find itself in the service of destructive forces. Think of the perverse eloquence of Nazi propaganda, bellowing horrors through loudspeakers. Are these disciplines, then, to become weapons of mass destruction or arts which we can all use in a constructive way? It's up to us to choose. This is why the arts of speech absolutely need to be grounded in speech in the full sense of the term.

The conception defended here is novel in two ways. First of all, these seven disciplines have never before been put together and treated as part of a single, conceptually distinct, enterprise: the arts of speech. The second novelty is in the teleological conception which underlies the unitary treatment: what holds the seven disciplines together is a crucial mission which is clearly defined, that of restoring the value of speech as a way of creating connections between people. This is a common good which is the foundation of our humanity and our dignity as persons.

### Three domains. Where worlds intersect

Starting from these assumptions, I recognize the following seven arts of speech: theatre, narrative, poetry, eloquence, oral presentation, dialogue, debate. The arts of speech stand at the place where the worlds of the artist, the intellectual, and the citizen touch and overlap.

All the arts of speech structure the sensible and create sense, using it as material. They are arts which make things present in the very moment at which they are practised. They aspire to make a deep impact, but one based on a complementarity of speaking and listening. They are living arts that bring people together by embodying something and by providing interpretations of important aspects of human life. They are the arts of speaking, acting, and being, of time, of the Other, and of establishing and cultivating connections between people.

One can evaluate the achievements of the arts of speech along three dimensions:

- *creation* (that is, *original production* in literature): theatre, narrative, poetry
- *transmission*, used now in a specific positive sense, as the passing on of something in a particular context: oral presentations, eloquence
- *interaction*: the exchange of ideas: dialogue, debate.

This tripartite division is an idealization based on the characteristic basic gesture of each of the arts in question; it is not intended to be a strait-jacket which will confine each one of them narrowly to a limited domain. Obviously each art, in its own distinctive way, integrates all three spheres: the artistic, the intellectual, and the civic. Each one encompasses all of the three dimensions: creation, transmission, interaction. This by no means implies that the relative emphasis given to each of these dimensions will be the same in every one. After all, each one has its own specific set of values and priorities. For instance, in the case of a debate, interaction will tend to outweigh creation. In oral presentation, on the other hand, transmission will generally take precedence over interaction.

### Seven arts. The whole spectrum of speech

The logic that operates here is one of complementarity, in that each art brings its own specific contribution to speech, and the mutual support of these seven arts is what constitutes the richness of the domain of speech, taken as a whole.

*Theatre* is the art of *speech incarnate*. The art of presence, of immediate encounters, of listening. The art of the actor, the stage, the troupe, of playing, of the '*live*' performance, of the public (in general) and the audience (in particular), of people who have come together to watch and listen. It is the art of the present because those assembled share the same present moment, here and now.

*Narrative* is the art of *speech reported*, of story-telling, of describing an entire world, inventing a universe, creating characters, exploring possibilities, constructing a plot, all with the intention of drawing the audience into the story. This category includes all forms of narrative, stories, tales, sagas, myths.

*Poetry* is the art of *displaced or off-centre speech*. It is concerned with the decentring of language, the change of register or context, of invention and metamorphosis. It is the art of opening language up in all directions, and letting it exalt in its own power. It allows anyone who recites it and anyone who is open to it to understand what is essential and see the impossible. Poetry is incantation, music, vertiginous mystery. It includes epic, song-texts, rap, and slam.

*Eloquence* is the art of *effective speech which has an impact.* It is the art of speaking well, and of speech enhanced by the use of rhetorical techniques, of effective speech which makes an impact on those who listen to it. It has as its goal to present a position and argue a case, to convince, to please, to move, to persuade. It encompasses elocution and all the arts of oratory.

*Oral presentation* is the art of *informative speech* which is devoted to transmitting ideas, disseminating forms of knowledge, formulating points of view, and putting them into the optimal shape to make them accessible to an audience. It is a way of sharing knowledge and giving people a taste for it. It includes the art of summarizing, and of formal and informal instruction.

*Dialogue* is the art of *interactive speech* in which different agents share their views with each other. The participants in a dialogue exchange words and glances rather than blows. They are speaking to each other, listening to what the Other says and responding, without trying to emerge victorious from the encounter or to persuade the other person, without trying to get the better of their interlocutor or pull the audience over to their side. The category of 'dialogue' includes the conversation, the exchange of views, the informal chat, the interview.

*Debate* is the art of *confrontational speech.* This is the art of being able to oppose given points of view and thereby make one's own prevail, of knowing how to press one's arguments, rally support for them, deal with objections, win over the audience. It includes the formal verbal sparring match, various types of polemics, and verbal argumentation for or against a given proposal.

These seven arts are essentially complementary and they form, as it were, all the keys in which the human instrument can play. Taken together they can express all the human harmonies we are capable of.

*A coherent unity. Fully realized humanity*

This unitary array of seven arts, which links creation, trans-mission, and interaction, also maps out a living path which speech can follow. One can see it as a kind of global track along which humanity can progress, deploying the appropriate art at the appropriate time and place. One could think of this as constituting something like a coherent, unitary life-cycle for speech, like the succession of days in the week or the sequence of notes in a musical scale. In this sense, speech must invent itself and its form with poetry. It must grow and develop with narrative, it gives itself corporeal form and a concrete sense of its audience with the theatre. Eloquence permits it to present itself in its most attractive and effective way. Speech attains clear formulation and is passed on in oral presentation, and when different people engage in dialogue, speech is exchanged and enriched. In debate, speakers are forced to take a position, stand up for themselves, and confront opposing views. Speech lives through being cultivated in the seven arts, and it will die if they are neglected.

The arts of speech in this sense encompass all the aspects of the great adventure we are engaged in, that of trying to become truly human, and it integrates them – our relation to the world, to ourselves, and to others – into a single dynamic. Speech is something we must construct and perfect by putting together these complementary approaches following the blueprints pro-vided by these seven arts. We do this in the interest of attaining a full and all-encompassing form of human experience and we use as our guide in the construction of a global conception of speech and an understanding of the human person as an organic unity. Both 'speech' and 'person' here are taken in an exceptionally wide sense as including all their aspects.

The consequence of all this is that mastering the ensemble of the seven arts of speech is a way of realizing our humanity along all its multiple dimensions. Only by doing this do we become the authors of our own speech, and capable of keeping our given word and acting on it. Otherwise we end up as mere objects pinned down by what others say, or we are at best speaking like battery chickens who have been so stuffed full of other people's messages that we begin to dribble them out of our own mouths again. Cultivating the seven arts is learning to engage in the right kind of responsible speech, and acquiring the ability to form bonds with other people. Practising these arts means embracing fully creation, live presentation to an audience, and interaction, which form the heart of our humanity, and distinguishing them from other phenomena with which they are often confused – mere self-expression, broadcasting, and confrontation. There is actually a huge difference between creation and mere self-expression – not everything that anyone ever says is worth saying. Broadcasting something *at* a potential audience is completely different from presenting it *to* them. Finally, to confront someone is to stand opposed to them, which is not the same as interacting *with* them. The goal of the seven arts is to permit us to make the shift from being mere broadcasters of our own opinion to being interlocutors with other people. The arts of speech allow us to enter into relation with others; they create, sustain, and nourish bonds between us; they vitalize them and contribute to creating a widely shared network of human links.

As I have already said, speech is simply a fact about humans, but it must also be seen as a unified whole. Each of the arts of speech expresses one of the essential constituents of this totality. If one wishes to speak correctly and well, to speak *with* others and connect with them, it is crucial to be able to integrate the seven arts in a variety of ways, varying according to the situation. The process of mastering each of these arts is one which requires sustained application, concentration, and practice. There is in principle no end to this learning process, but also no limit to how far one can go in perfecting one's skills. Mastering these arts and exercising them attentively in a way which is responsive to their symbiotic relation to each other and to the needs of the situation in which they are being used can give rise to 'right speech' – speech in the full sense of the term which is responsible, establishes and intensifies bonds, creates meaning, and is a basic vehicle of our humanity.

## An iconoclastic choice. A modern septet

### *Freeing oneself from arbitrary demarcations*

So we have, then, theatre, narrative, poetry, eloquence, oral presentation, dialogue, debate. The choice of precisely these seven elements as constituting collectively the arts of speech is justified by reference to the inherent teleological structure, the recognized capacities, the actual effect, and the contribution each one can make, when combined with the others in an appropriate way, to attaining the absolute goal: the realization of speech in the full and undiminished sense. Consequently, in making my selection, I have intentionally ignored disciplinary boundaries, the established distinctions between genres, the customary classifications, and the classic hierarchies between subjects. The urgency of the task at hand requires us to move the existing frontiers and go beyond the usual lines of demarcation. We need to transform the way in which we conceive of the different disciplines in order to allow their true sense to emerge more clearly and connect them more intimately with action. We must mobilize all the living forces which they embody and use them to form alliances that energize us and allow us to transcend and overcome existing differences between groups. In this sense, all people of good will are welcome to join us and all the means that can be employed in a genuinely useful way are acceptable. Aragon wrote during the Occupation, calling for a federation of all those willing to resist, even those who belonged to opposing factions,

*Quand les blés sont sous la grêle*
*Fou qui fait le délicat*
*Fou qui songe à ses querelles*
*Au cœur du commun combat.*

[When the hail is falling on the crops/ Only a fool has time for delicacy of sentiment/ When the common struggle rages/ Only a fool thinks of his private quarrels.][3]

In view of all this, it should come as no surprise that, in a way that might initially seem counterintuitive, I do not automatically include among the arts of speech all the disciplines and theories belonging to the human sciences (for instance, philosophy and psychoanalysis), the techniques that have been developed for personal development (coaching), procedures aimed at providing spiritual comfort (confession), professional legal or paralegal practices (social counselling, negotiation, arbitration, conciliation) – although all of these are founded on speech and each has a fundamental, if only partial, contribution to make to the flourishing of our seven arts of speech.

My prospectus of the arts of speech does not therefore aspire to be absolutely exhaustive of every form of human undertaking that helps us to cultivate our speech-centred humanity; to try to do this would simply result in an infinite list that would be of no practical value. If I had to enumerate all the crafts, practices, and human activities that have theorical roots in speech, all the hours of the day would not be enough, and even undertaking that task would itself be a way of continuing to wallow in the degradation of speech which characterizes our modern world. That would be the end of any hope of revitalizing speech, and with it any hopes we might have had of a subsequent regeneration of our own human condition. Thousands of pages would not be enough to list all the relevant phenomena, and the basic conception I wish to defend would get completely lost in the details.

So I wish to try to look beyond the specifics of particular professions or disciplines (the rhetorical technique of the lawyer, the pedagogical methods of the university lecturer) and focus on the common factors and the features that lie at the root of all these practices and have given them and continue to give them a stable foundation; not, of course, that any of these activities could be fully reduced to what is contained in that foundation. This is true not just for monologic disciplines, but also for dialogue and debate, whether they are social, philosophical, political, or journalistic. These seven arts of speech, therefore, contribute to the greater flourishing of all the domains of human activity, all the spaces of collective human interaction. One does not need to be a professional artist to recognize the importance of joining in to support this project.

## Clearing up this dog's dinner

The fact that the grouping of these seven arts together is somewhat eclectic has some significant implications. To start with, dialogue and debate are considered to be arts on the same terms as theatre or poetry. Categorizing them in this way, however, means rethinking the value we usually attribute to them. Integrating them into the body of the arts of speech is not uncontroversial, but rather means taking a distinctive position on them. This is intentional and marks a reaction against the radically debased state in which those two 'formats' – dialogue and debate – find themselves in the electronic multimedia free-for-all which the public space has become. We are in a state in which dialogue and debate are confused, and debate finds itself on a slippery slope to perdition in that it has become increasingly difficult to distinguish it clearly from confrontation. Confrontation becomes, then, increasingly a matter of polemics designed to annihilate the person with whom one is speaking.

To affirm that debate and dialogue are forms of art is to demand we raise them, once again, to that status, by giving them back a full sense of their own power, so that they can be re-established in their former dignity. This is part of what it means to differentiate them and recognize them as two distinct activities, not to treat them as a pair of indistinguishable clones, but as a fraternal grouping of two brother arts, each with its own specific aims, despite their shared heritage. Differentiating them is the only way to prevent dialogue from being thrown into the meat-grinder of 'debate' (falsely so called), so that variety, nuance, and structure are completely destroyed and everything that is said is just mashed together, ultra-processed, and dished out in tiny bite-size portions, to which one's interlocutor must give an immediate, equally undifferentiated response. The result is a gloopy, indigestible mess of verbiage. We need to put an end to this.

This is to say that debate and dialogue both depend on principles, values, methods, and forms of cognition which are nowadays neglected, denigrated, despised, and suppressed. In fact, at their best, dialogue and debate obey the same rules that art does. These rules give priority to the values of reciprocity; they attempt to ensure that representatives of different positions properly engage with one another's points of view, that violence is overcome, that interlocutors do not simply dismiss the opinions of their opponents summarily, that antagonisms are limited and focused on relevant disagreements, that all positions are given a hearing, and that no one simply disqualifies the views they disagree with simply as strange, absurd, motivated by hostility, or not worthy of discussion. When I speak, then, of elevating dialogue and discussion to the level of fine arts, I am implicitly indicting the present abysmal state in which we find ourselves with regard to these two central human practices, and also indicating how far we have to go to reach our full potential.

### Embodying all the genres of literature

Dialogue and debate are arts of interaction; that is why I adopt the heterodox view of insisting upon including them among the seven arts of speech. As far as the three arts of creation are concerned – poetry, narrative, and theatre – the reason for their inclusion is a more standard and widely recognized one: they explicitly arise from three modern literary genres: the poem, the story, and the drama. It was Victor Hugo who formulated this triad at the beginning of the nineteenth century in his famous manifesto of romanticism, the *Preface to Cromwell*. Hugo was following the lead of the German philosopher Schelling, who distinguished lyric subjectivity, epic objectivity, and drama, with the latter as a synthesis of the former two forms: in other words, the art of 'I' (alone), the art of 'she, he, and they', and the art of 'I/you/we'.[4]

For Hugo, this trichotomy has a historical dimension in that the poem is eventually displaced by the story, which then in turn is superseded by drama. I would like to retain the trichotomy as an analytical tool, but without adopting the theory of evolution associated with it. In particular, I do not wish to endorse Hugo's messianic idea that there was a dialectical movement of thesis/antithesis/synthesis operating through history: 'Poetry has three ages, each of which corresponds to a state of society: the poem, the narrative, the drama. Primitive times are lyrical, ancient times epic, and modern times dramatic. The poem sings of eternity, the epic narrative solemnizes history, and drama depicts life.'[5] Despite the seductiveness of this view, I don't wish to introduce this kind of hierarchy among the different genres.

This tripartite division of types of literary creation is fundamental to modernity, and it has endured up to the present day, in the form of the distinction which still structures our thinking about the major genres: poetry, theatre, and the novel. If one looks at them from the point of view of the arts of speech, one can see that all three of these genres have a natural bias toward live performance: theatrical pieces are really themselves when they are actually produced, presented, and played by real actors; stories when they are recounted by a speaker to a live audience; poetry when it is recited aloud. Obviously, these genre-based categories (poetry, narrative, theatre) are just as permeable as the three modalities of speech (creation, communication, interaction), because literature is free and infinitely fertile in generating new forms which violate all existing conventions, and in throwing up hybrid forms, combinatorial possibilities, and mixtures, such as narrative theatre, dramatic epic, poetic drama, and so on.

### Impact must not outweigh cognition. Redressing the balance

Turning, then, from the arts of creation and interaction, it remains to justify the inclusion of the art of transmission. Eloquence seems to fit into the ensemble of arts of speech in a very natural way, because it is precisely the art of finding formulations that are aimed at being maximally effective; it is the art of transmitting messages so that they have palpable effects. It constitutes one of the seven arts of speech, but should not be construed as the essence of all of them – which of course in no way prevents speech from mobilizing all the resources and the power of rhetoric, if appropriate. Including eloquence among the arts of speech means recognizing its importance, not consecrating its hegemony over them all; it is quite distinct from the arts of creation and should neither dominate them nor subsume them into itself. Not only is eloquence not the whole story when it comes to performing works of literature, but it should itself be seen as a subgenre of performance. The proof of this is that sermons, eulogies, orations, and speeches themselves are established literary genres.

This very strongly suggests that we should recognize eloquence as having the dignity and nobility of an art, but deny that status to that miserable lilliputian avatar of eloquence which dominates our contemporary world, 'public speaking'. This is a pathetic ersatz version of something which was for a very long time – from antiquity to the twentieth century, from Demosthenes to Martin Luther King, Hypatia to Gandhi, Cicero to Louise Michel, and Winston Churchill to Simone Veil – the grand art form *par excellence*, the art of an oratory that rose to the demands which History itself placed upon it. If one judges our present situation by this standard, it is clear that we would profit enormously by extracting ourselves and keeping our distance from this era of insignificance, raising our sights, and trying to inaugurate a new age of eloquence.[6]

Recognizing oral presentation as the seventh art of speech is intended to mark its difference from eloquence in the usual sense. The essential characteristic of eloquence is its persuasiveness, but oral presentation has a fundamentally cognitive and pedagogical orientation and these take precedence over the needs of persuasion. An oral presentation in the sense intended here has a tacit commitment to transmitting knowledge, and this is not reducible to the desire to convince the audience to adopt any particular view, attitude, or course of action. It is a vehicle for cognition, not simply convictions. And no, not all purported cognition is simply personal conviction disguising itself as objective fact. If one held this view, one would also have to maintain that the whole of reality was nothing but a subjective illusion and truth did not exist, as if the universe depended simply on what I believe. To teach is, among other things, to try to persuade, but it is not *only* an attempt to persuade. There is always a content which instruction is trying to transmit, a content to which it is trying to make a contribution. Think of those teachers who are not satisfied with filling the minds of their listeners, but also try to set them on fire. The best teachers – those whom one remembers for the rest of one's life – are smugglers of incendiary material, of fundamental conceptions and modes of speech. They are people to whom I owe, to a large extent, what I am.

## From the liberal to the liberating arts

The seven arts integrate the essential dimensions of speech – creation, transmission, and interaction – but not in a way that obliterates differences. Rather, these arts allow us to integrate in an articulated way the aesthetic, the cognitive, the pragmatic, the ethical, and the political aspects of our lives - the beautiful, the true, the expedient, the good, and the just. One should not, then, confuse any of these arts with some other one: the theatre is not just the realm of dialogue or debate, debate is not in all cases dialogue, and not every dialogue is dramatic, just as not every poem is eloquent, and a narrative is not in itself automatically an oral presentation.

One can argue that oral presentation, dialogue, and debate are 'really' nothing more than sub-categories of eloquence. Verlaine tried in his '*ars poetica*' to separate poetry and eloquence in an irrevocable way, when he wrote: 'Take eloquence and wring its neck',[7] but one could even hold, contrary to this, that eloquence is the precondition of all the arts of speech, including poetry. Or one could follow the lead of the director Antoine Vitez, who wanted to 'make everything into theatre',[8] on the grounds that theatre could, by its own efforts, swallow up all the other forms of speech, from poetry to dialogue: just look at the dialogues of Plato, which are dramas of ideas, or the verses of the *Cid*,[9] which have lyrical power even within the context of a tragi-comedy. Finally, one could claim that poetry, in the original Greek sense of *poiesis*[10] – literary production, the art of creating, formulating, and shaping structures composed of words – is at the foundation of all verbal expression, or at least of any expression that has a 'style' and is thus a part of literature. After all, Gustave Flaubert has a 'poetics' as much as Nathalie Sarraute or Aimé Césaire does.

I admit that I have made a choice in selecting exactly these seven arts, and, since every art is a construct, I also admit that I have constructed these seven in a particular way, construing them as the framework for improving the quality of speech. This modern septet is also meant to be contrasted with the traditional seven liberal arts which were the basic subjects of instruction in antiquity and the Middle Ages. This traditional curriculum encompassed the *trivium* (the three subjects of grammar, rhetoric, and dialectic) and the *quadrivium* (arithmetic, geometry, music, and astronomy). This course of study instructed the beginning student in the power of language, ratio, and number. The *trivium* and the *quadrivium* taken together constituted seven 'paths' (*viae*) which mapped out the territory of objects that were very different from each other: words, numbers, shapes, celestial bodies, notes of music. In contrast, the seven arts we have been discussing in this work all treat the same object – speech – but without restricting that to spoken language or limiting the 'power' that these arts confer on a single kind of ability. Of course, in one sense, these seven arts are not even limited to speech, because they include theatre, which has a spoken component, but is not exhausted by that (or which, in some cases, even tries to free itself from the hegemony of the spoken word). What all our seven arts have in common, though, is that speech forms the keystone which gives them stability and structure. Just as in the case of the traditional seven liberal arts, they explore relations and establish bonds with other people. One difference is that the former arts include forms of cognition directed at nature (such as astronomy) whereas the latter are all concerned with human beings – in their relations to themselves, to others, and to the world. The arts of speech are in their very essence arts of humanity – liberating arts.

## The essential path of development.
## A heptathlon with humanity as the prize

*Cultivating knowledge, experience, and performance*

To progress through the seven arts of speech is to form bonds in a number of respects. Acquiring and cultivating the arts of speech is a way of getting into connection with the world, and this means moving out from oneself and then back via the Other, and also moving from any one given Other to a number of different Others via oneself. Learning to practise these arts proceeds through a number of successive stages: the first encounter, the awakening of interest, discovery, exploration, familiarization, deepening of skill and knowledge, all the way up to complete mastery. Those who take this path must be prepared to advance on three related tracks at the same time, first by learning techniques, methods, and skills and assimilating intimately the rules of whatever art is in question; second, by observing real performances carefully, which give a direct contact with the various forms of that art; and finally by putting one's experiences to use, that is, by actually practising the art. To put it in a slightly different way, one must form and educate oneself, learn to understand, and learn to experiment. One can do this only by coming to grasp the basic principles of the art, encountering work that shows it at its best, and trying to create something oneself.

To assimilate the rules of art, then, means to train oneself in the arts of speech. This process begins with one's entry into school and continues for the whole time one continues one's education. To be sure, our new conception means that one must rethink 'education in the arts' in an extensive, organic, and holistic way, expanding its domain to include, where appropriate for the particular case, all seven of the arts of speech. This means more than merely making some gestures, such as sprinkling some theatrical stardust, as a distraction, on a few very restricted parts of the educational programme. Or parachuting some kind of pseudo-comprehensive oral examination into the requirements for successful conclusion of secondary education, while actually doing nothing concrete to prepare pupils for it during the decade or so they spend in school. Instead, one should be trying to equip them with the skills that will allow each one of them to realize the best of themselves, to speak for themselves, and to stand up for what they say.

To attend performances thoughtfully means to enter into contact with works brought to life by artists of speech. What I mean by a 'work' in the realm of the arts of speech is a performance which is of high quality and demands the attention of the audience and the artists involved, one in which speech in its fullest sense manifests itself to a listening and observing individual or a group. Examples would be hearing and seeing a play, a recital of poetry, or a rap concert. But I would also include such things as following an oral presentation with appropriate attention, taking part in a dialogue, or listening to a debate, provided that the presentation, dialogue, or debate in question satisfied the requirements which I have described for instantiating the general art of speech. Precisely because it is true that one learns best from examples, it is all the more urgent that we promote the arts of speech in our societies in order to provide appropriate models to learn from.

Practising the seven arts of speech requires experimentation at all levels. This means trying things out with past masters of speech and with amateurs, with recognized senior practitioners of some art, with lay persons, and with recognized experts, with people of all of these kinds and sometimes all mixed in together. This should take place in ludic, professional, strictly experimental, private, public, and hybrid contexts. For dialogue and debate, this means forcing oneself to respect the rules of art without yielding to the temptation to start down the slippery slope which ends with the participants pounding each other to pieces. Rather, one should follow the advice of Gide and impose on oneself the discipline 'to follow one's inclination, provided it leads one up hill'.[11] One should cultivate speech in all its dimensions, engaging, like an athlete of speech, in a variety of different practices and experimenting with all seven of the arts. Mastering speech is like winning the heptathlon, and it is precisely the synergy that arises when all seven arts of speech are practised together in a disciplined way that opens the path that leads to the realization of our full humanity.

We also need to learn to enter into texts, to internalize them, but also to embody them, because texts, in addition to orally articulated behaviour and to the use of sign language, constitute one of the two sources of speech. Texts are written speech, received and passed down through the centuries from a series of authors each of whom had a powerful voice. These writers form the framework within which literature is created – it does not spring up spontaneously from nowhere, for instance from improvisation, but rather it represents speech that has been worked on. In addition, the more authentic, genuine, essential speech we have been exposed to, the more capable we shall become of ourselves producing new forms of such speech, when our time comes. This, too, is something that can and must be learned. There are a few exceptions to this rule of thumb, to be sure. On the other hand, not everyone who claims to be the new Rimbaud is actually a Rimbaud, and it by no means diminishes Rimbaud's genius to note that before becoming a poet at the age of seventeen, he won a prize at the age of fifteen for Latin composition. Education is not the enemy of inspiration; it is, rather, a resource to be utilized.

### Speech sets the limits within which humanity can exist

What, then, is the final goal of this system of seven arts of speech? To establish connections with other people, to enrich and enhance the life we live, to allow us to transcend ourselves, to bring reconciliation. What do we need in order to live together in a society at peace with itself and others, to bring the city together, and to realize a world of liberty, equality, and fraternity? We need to tolerate and even seek out the presence of others, and we need to listen to them. We need shared narrative and genuine dialogue. We need to be able to make sense of the world and to understand nuances in human behaviour. We need authenticity, beauty, and truth. Also love, benevolence, humour, and dignity. We need encounters with others based on mutual respect. We need to learn to pay attention, to master skills, to do the right thing in the right circumstances. We need to express ourselves, and to do this in sophisticated ways. We need emotional outlets, ways of explaining ourselves to others; we need to be able to act out what we are, to realize ourselves by sublimating ourselves, and to acquire a sense of self-achievement.

We need humanity.

Everything, that is, that the seven arts of speech, each in its own unique way, bring us and offer to share with us.

That is not to say that mastery of speech is in itself enough. Where war rages, in the face of massive crimes, massacres, destruction on a grand scale, humanitarian catastrophes, one must act and resist unchained violence, the violence that understands only itself and will not listen to reason. Here there is no place for naïveté; human beings are not angels. To desire peace and work toward reconciliation is in no sense to deny the necessity of fighting, when that is what must be done, where there is no alternative. In such contexts, the political pursuit of peace at all costs becomes appeasement and can spiral out of control into capitulation, as in Munich in 1938. If, as is certainly the case, diplomacy is an art, and one based on dialogue, nevertheless, it takes place in a context in which war is always possible, no matter how ardently the diplomat seeks peace.

I simply remark at this point that, when Russia invaded Ukraine on 22 February 2022, a hero of resistance who stood up for liberty suddenly emerged, apparently from nowhere. To the amazement of the rest of the world, this was the Ukrainian President Volodymyr Zelensky. Nothing in his past would have seemed to have prepared him for this role, as President in time of war and champion of resistance – nothing except that he had been an actor who by a strange coincidence had success-fully played the role of a chief of state, accidentally thrust into that position by an election held under highly unusual circum-stances. Rather than being surprised that in this case reality is as strange as fiction, one ought to be moved to note how exactly fiction in this case prefigured reality. We can see here what it means for speech in its full sense to be instantiated; mastery of speech in this case allowed a powerful tribune of the people to emerge. It would be a mistake to trivialize this and say that Zelensky is 'merely' a good 'communicator'. It is part of our contemporary dilemma that it even occurs to anyone to think this, and it shows the debasement of our conception of 'communication'. The public relations sense of 'commu-nication' is nothing but the shadow of what it really could be – what it really is. Words are not just a matter of image. Speech cannot be reduced to a sequence of shiny tit-bits, easily quotable items, sound-bites. This is all an instance of what Debord called the 'society of spectacle', a place of constant war where one falsehood is always on the offensive against another. What is sure is that we have passed from a civilization based on meanings to one based on the 'communication' produced by public relations experts.

In this regard, 'following the talking points' is a grotesque caricature of narrative, just as the slogan is a degenerate avatar of poetry. The televised spectacular is the poor cousin of the play properly performed in a theatre, and the punchline the putrifying residue left when eloquence has passed away. Jargon-ridden talks in Globish or business-speak are a sinister imitation of proper oral presentations, and the fluent, unilat-eral monopolization of the discussion by one of the parties is the exact reverse of a dialogue. The polemical clash which never ends is the terrible negation of debate. In the *Republic*, Plato describes the degeneration of political regimes into morbid versions of themselves. Democracy becomes demagogy, aristocracy becomes oligarchy, and monarchy ends up as tyranny.[12] We find ourselves today in a similar situation with regard to speech: it has degenerated in almost all its forms. We are, all of us, the only ones who can regenerate it, but only by trying to revivify the arts of speech in their full range, and this can be accomplished only by real action.

# 7

# The Centre for the Arts of Speech

## Embodiment

### *Realizing speech in the full sense*

As a response to the radical degradation of speech, I propose trying to re-elevate it through the cultivation of the arts of speech. Given the importance of what is at stake here, this must be accompanied by a plan for concrete action to put this process into effect. With this in mind, I assembled a team of artists and other skilled practitioners of the arts of speech, plucking them from their separate spheres and uniting them in a novel common cause: I created the Centre for the Arts of Speech. Its goal is to allow us to improve our ability to speak and establish relations with one another, rather than trying to kill each other off. I and my associates and collaborators wish to promote a humanism of speech. By giving people access to speech in the strong sense of the term, we wish to educate and transform them, but also to bring them together and allow them to enlighten each other.

Together, we are establishing this Centre for the Arts of Speech as an artistic, intellectual, and civic enterprise with both a national and an international dimension, a project not

only for native speakers of French, but also for all the citizens
of our multilingual world. Our Centre initiates a new movement in that it is a space devoted entirely to the arts of speech.
All these arts will be deployed in the interests of humanity and
social reconciliation for the goal of elevating speech: that is, of
enabling it to pursue its task of creating meaning and getting
beyond violence. It is in this spirit that we unite in this space
the seven arts of speech, as we conceive them: theatre, narrative, poetry, eloquence, oral presentation, dialogue, debate.
The Centre we wish to create will be a space of creation, but
also of transmission and debate, a space for experimenting,
and for attempting to understand and improve speech, for
restoring its true value. We want the idea that our society
can be a 'Republic' – something 'shared in common by all the
citizens' – to be not merely an empty phrase, but a living reality, a reality created and maintained in existence by speaking
correctly and justly, by keeping our word once we have given
it, and by acting in accordance with what we say.

## Making speech central

We intend that our Centre for the Arts of Speech will have a
very broad remit and we also take its name literally. We wish to
create a physical space where projects can come into focus and
be realized, a place with a vibrant present where the immediate
presence of Others can be experienced. A welcoming space
which concentrates attention on the ways in which different
people and groups can encounter each other so that meaning
is created. We wish to invite people in to a forum where different paths cross, and from which they may emerge transformed.

Speech, thought, and debate on the substantial issues that
confront us all should have their place here. Here one can
listen to the songs of the poets, the thunder-and-lightning of
history, and the voice of the world. Here questions become
living reality, spirits respond when they are invoked, different

points of view draw themselves up and confront each other, and perspectives run together. The crises of our historical moment, the burning issues that divide us, the works of the past that have stood the test of time, they all can reveal themselves here. This will occur in debates, dialogues, workshops, organized encounters, performances, and other creative collective projects which will be based on collaboration between different arts and cooperation between people with different kinds of talents. We aspire to mobilize creative energies in order to produce a series of fusions of different imaginary domains in our real physical space.

We wish the Centre to be a place from which ideas radiate effectively so that they actually change people's lives and influence the way they think and act. We wish to encourage a kind of thinking that will be agile yet engaged, that will easily cross existing borders, but also be invested in the situation in which it finds itself, and we wish it to be present in all the domains of speech. It must be open to encounters in all the worlds that humans inhabit, ready for any nomadic adventure which reality throws our way. We wish to extend the reach of speech everywhere, to make its contact with reality more substantial, to teach people to listen to what others say and share their viewpoints, to enable them to embark on any road that leads to other people. In the Centre, the arts of speech will be a living reality; they will exhibit all their power, as we promote, cultivate, integrate, and transmit them locally, nationally, and internationally, leaping over existing barriers and ignoring frontiers. We shall build bridges and establish links between individuals and groups, despite their differences and despite the distance that exists between them. Through the vitality of speech, wherever it takes place, people will be able to share a present with each other.

Here or elsewhere. We shall experience this vivid presence in each of us and between all of us.

## *Giving the civic realm concrete existence*

We are creating this Centre for the Arts of Speech as a public space, for everyone and for the city, infusing it with the spirit of decentralization. This means, among other things, construing the theatre as a 'public service' (Vilar),[1] a 'form of elitism open to all' (Vitez).[2] We wish to assemble and put together 'all manner of things for everyone' (Hugo),[3] to offer excellence to all, to demonstrate that forms of speech can at the same time be both demanding and fully intelligible; can be accessible and can yet move beyond our existing forms of thought and feeling. That meaning can be shared and can be felt to be shared. A spirit of openness will pervade the Centre, as will a willingness to influence others and be influenced by them.

We wish to create a Centre *for* the city, a place where one can encounter diverse people and respect their differences. Thus we envisage something which is the absolute antithesis of the existing machines for denigrating others and negating them by reducing them to stereotypes. In contrast, the Centre will take account of the specific individuality of others and value them for who they are, recognizing them as beings endowed with the power of speech. The intention will be to encourage the formation of a society of people who speak with one another, in which each person is recognized as the *alter ego* of each of the others, and each one has a full right to a voice. We see this as a way in which violence can be restrained and kept in limits. The Centre will provide a framework within which by virtue of exploring, becoming familiar with, learning, practising, and mastering the arts of speech, people will become able to sublimate and go beyond themselves.

We will create a space in the heart of the city devoted to contributing to the cultivation of civic responsibility by bringing different communities and publics together, and allowing them to reflect on themselves. We propose to do this by asking questions that will help us to refine our social consciences. We wish our Centre to express our own age, but also to connect us with other ages, a place where stories are told, different cultures appreciated, and thoughts are crystallized, where people can assemble and democracy can be enacted, a secure harbour for citizens who are devoted to the common good and recognize their mission and vocation to make culture accessible to all. Our ideal is the citizen who has fallen in love with language as a common resource shared by all humans, who loves the multiplicity of languages as a part of the spiritual inheritance of humanity, and who loves words as a universal treasure.

The Centre will be a place in which people meet, a bulwark against the solitude which withers us, the withdrawal into the self which destroys us. Because we need to speak to one another, listen to one other, and understand one another, and this must take place *'live'* in the real immediate presence of the Other. More than ever, we need speech: to express ourselves, to communicate, to transmit our knowledge, to persuade others of our point of view, to reflect, to create, to come together and find unity and reconciliation with our peers. This is what our Centre is about. We wish to create a living space where people can come together by learning to speak to each other, a place where speech is revealed as the medium *par excellence* through which humans relate to each other, and where it demonstrates that it can have a real effect.

## Starting to speak with the world

More than ever, the world speaks to us through thousands of languages. It should be inspiring for us to hear them. So, although it is true that the Centre for the Arts of Speech is anchored in the world of French speech, we construe it very much as a cosmopolitan and multilingual space, a place where one can hear any number of different languages – European, African, Asian, American, Polynesian – a crossroads where all forms of speech have a place and a right of expression, and where many diverse nationalities will be able to experience the pride which comes from hearing themselves speak publicly in their own voice, while also discovering the voices of their neighbours.

We understand our Centre as a crossroads in an expansive sense: a place where languages overlap should also be a place which is open to the world and authentically international, a place where different peoples, cultures, and traditions meet, where different worlds encounter each other, where different communities discover each other and learn to respect and accept each other's idiosyncrasies and differences, but also to recognize their complementarities. We wish to promote diversity, multicultural exchange, and fruitful interaction; coexistence, mutual understanding, and tolerance. Finally, a crossroads is a place where local initiatives and international adventures can come into contact with each other, and where the diversity of the world can manifest itself and make itself present in all its various forms.

## *Making a pact with the digital*

For all that, our Centre is not part of a reactionary struggle designed to turn back the clock in the name of living speech. We do not wish to return to the *ancien régime* of the Word, to those past epochs dominated by the oral, the written, or the printed – the logosphere or the graphosphere, as Régis Debray puts it.[4] The world before the digital revolution is not our world; quite the contrary. We wholeheartedly welcome the unlimited and unprecedented opportunities and possibilities which the new technologies open up. We intend to make use of them, to cultivate them, and to deploy them fully. They represent an inspiration to us and a challenge which we accept. They transform us, and we change ourselves through our engagement with them. We hope to intervene in them, to use them in our creative processes, and to make our mark in them. Obviously, in one sense, *homo digitalis* is *homo deus* raised, by the internet, to the nth power. By the same token, it is that much more important to prevent the abuses to which the electronic media can so easily lend themselves. It would be a distortion of our position to present it as if it were based on a straightforward confrontation between speech and the digital, a kind of despairing reaction against triumphant modernity, or an up-to-date version of the old *Querelle des Anciens et des Modernes*. We have no intention of falling into the trap of thinking that we are engaged in a Manichaean war between smug technophiles and traumatized technophobes.

We envisage a pact between speech and the digital in which our Centre combines the best from each of the two worlds, using the written word – a third world – as the bridge between the two. We wish to appropriate and cultivate the immense power which has been unleashed by the digital revolution, while at the same time reversing one of the characteristics of this revolution, by re-establishing the primacy of the content over the medium. Speech – that is, the content of what is conceived, expressed, embodied, and directed at the auditor – comes first, then its digital realization, which makes it universally available. Speech is the origin and first principle, not merely a pure product or by-product of communication. We are not Luddites, nor do we take Don Quixote as our model ('Down with all screens!'). Neither, however, are we techno-fanatics ('The screen *über alles!*'). We are not willing to retreat to a ghetto of like-minded *aficionados*, nor are we willing to put up with the degradation of speech in the public domain; these, we think, would be two sides of the very same catastrophe.

## Action

Our aim in creating the Centre for the Arts of Speech is to educate, transform, influence, and unite people – by means of speech. This means improving our speech, teaching people to understand it better, to master it, and to be able to experiment with it, and enhancing our ability to deepen our relations with each other. This is what a cultivation of the arts of speech can do.

### Learning to understand. The meaning of speech

The Centre for the Arts of Speech was created as a space for debate and dialogue, where meaning can be articulated and speech can become more meaningful. We wish to promote thought in verbal interaction, the exchange of points of view, the sharing of reflections, the confrontation of different perspectives. We propose to do this by organizing events, lectures, informal chats, discussions, round tables, and debates in which we will explore the major issues of the present, the crises that are now occurring, the ideas that have a future. We wish to put together in a fruitful way experience and expertise, modes of seeing and forms of knowledge. Our message is that we must all learn to listen and try to understand each other, and that we must be concerned to cultivate rational argumentation. This we take to be the best way to develop and sharpen our critical capacities and to prevent them from deteriorating into a mere desire for confrontation. We need to struggle continually against the dangers of gullibility, the fanaticism engendered by prejudices, the poison of disinformation, and the madness of conspiracy theories. Against the tendency to make snap judgements based on stereotypes, we appeal to our ability to be sensitive to complexity. We reject the reductionism which sees every case as nothing but an instance of pre-given categories. We reject the pseudo-simplicity and conformism of thinking based on stereotypes. We reject the Manichaeanism which always divides the world into antagonistic groups. Most of all, we reject the blind condemnation of the Other which is a concomitant of this kind of thinking. Against the discourse of hatred, we invoke the art of dialogue, and against the call to civil war, we wish to mobilize meaningful debate. We need to learn to accept dynamic contradictions without confusing them with untenable antagonisms.

Our Centre must permit us to find a way to undertake concrete measures which will include literary and publishing activities; engagement with and in the media will allow us to advance our goals of understanding speech and to explain why it is important in a given context. We need to learn how to make the arts of speech relevant and influential. Books, essays, interviews, performances, public appearances, and statements: all of these are important, but there will be other modes of engagement, too, which we hope to discover.

### Setting up experiments. Staging speech

We envisage a space for creation and expression which will provide a framework and context for speech – actual concrete talking, timeless narratives, imaginative constructions, discussions of the facts, essential speculations about who and what we are, and about our situation. The Centre is to be a home for traffickers of texts who are keen to explore meaning in all its dimensions. It issues a perpetual invitation to learn to appreciate the intention behind any given proposal, the real significance of a certain discourse, and the force embodied in a way of thinking about things. We wish to arouse the critical spirit in people and encourage them to interpret what they hear. We wish to allow language to express itself in all its immediacy, its resonance, its power. In our Centre, oral speech will find a context for itself, written works will come alive, and narratives will proliferate. The Centre will help people to recreate the world in speech by fashioning stories, large-scale collective histories, personal autobiographies, distinctive individual tales, and universal narratives. We wish to explore all the registers, genres, and styles of speech. In the Centre, we shall move between disciplines, beyond the aesthetic, cultural, national, and linguistic barriers which separate artistic languages and idioms from each other. The Centre will be a workshop within which new forms of writing, conceiving, repeating, and presenting speech are associated with new and varied forms of action: odysseys, festivals, spectacles, performances, linguistic experiments, which draw on a wide range of novel human experience.

## Learning to master the power of speech

Our Centre is an educational space, in which skills can be acquired and developed, a place for exploring the nature, the riches, the power, and the import of speech. We wish to teach people to use speech in the right way: responsibly, reasonably, and so that it connects them concretely and actively with others. The kind of mastery which we envisage requires the integrated appropriation of all seven of the arts of speech: theatre, narrative, poetry, eloquence, oral presentation, dialogue, debate. Proper students of speech need to acquire the appropriate set of tools. They need to be able to elaborate, formalize, express themselves, argue, affirm, synthesize, free themselves from their prejudices, interact, and enter into social relations with others. Only then can they give their speech meaning, sense, effectiveness, power, and resonance.

We treat speech as a unitary, total phenomenon, approaching it in a global, structural, and systematic way. We encompass everything in our purview, from the original conception of an idea to its final embodiment, and from monologic discourse to language-mediated interaction. We study all the concrete permutations and forms speech can take, with the intention of developing our ability to listen and join with others in creating meaning. Our Centre wishes to help people to acquire for themselves that immediate physical 'presence' which is so admired in great actors. People who have mastered speech should be able to formulate their own thoughts, to stand up for them, to focus with others on the tasks at hand, thereby entering into positive relations with those others, and going out beyond themselves. This is something anyone can aspire to, male or female, young or old, elementary school pupils or retirees, no matter what one's status, whether one is a public servant or a private individual, an employee or a manager, an elected official or a teacher. The Centre can be of benefit to individuals or groups, to people who suffer from extreme glossophobia and wish to conquer it, to people already skilled in oral presentation and public speaking who wish to hone those skills, and to everyone in between.

Our Centre will focus on developing the general competences, the specific techniques, the know-how, and the skills which are essential for speaking effectively: the rational, the affective, the expressive, the creative, the practical, the constructive, the pragmatic, the interactive, and the social. It will do so by showing people directly how to deploy them and bringing them to bear on concrete situations. This will provide a solid foundation for speech, will give it life, and will make it effective.

## Organizing collaboration

### Defining the dimensions

We speak to each other in order to maintain our human connection. This is the basic rationale of the Centre for the Arts of Speech, and our goal is to demonstrate that it is the case. This is why we situate our activities at the intersection of a number of different dimensions, orienting ourselves in each on a clear axis.

We affirm that there is a vertical axis of the principles that should structure our societies: language as the base; the rule of law as the pedestal on which all else rests; culture as the soul; freedom as the spirit; the critical spirit as the general

precondition; secularism as the basic orientation; emancipa-
tion as the ultimate project; social peace as the immediate
goal; democratic debate as an imperative; and the forging of a
common destiny as our collective task.

We also actively embrace a horizontal axis of the various
force that animate our social life: the need for reciprocity and
equality of opportunity; the power of diversity; the multiplication of identities; the developing dialogue between different
cultures; the richness, recognition of truth, and respect for
others revealed in and through debate; the plurality of different
interpretations of the world, of texts, and of each other; the
acceptance of difference; and the need for tolerance.

There is, however, also a third axis, that of transversality,
which cuts across the previous two in that there are a number
of different logically consistent ways to put together the elements in our universe. We must cultivate a spirit of openness,
of multidisciplinarity and cultural diversity, take a chance on
intelligence, and recognize that people demand intelligibility
of speech and action in a world in which populations are amal-
gamating and generations mixing. In this world, we must place
our bets especially on the young.

## A Centre for all

We propose, then, to try to bring people together along these
three axes and unify them around the idea of speech as a
common good, and we wish to do so despite the fact that we
know that they are antecedently participants in a wide variety
of very different forms of speech. We believe that right speech
is a condition of our common humanity and the foundation of
our society, and that is why we address ourselves to all those
who make up our society.

We address ourselves to all citizens, to all those who have
a stake in robust, healthy speech; who want to understand, to
learn and to experiment, to change their relation to speech by

educating themselves in the arts of speech, in order to connect with themselves, with others, and with the world. Our Centre will be open to all those who wish to commit themselves to responsible speech, to finding once again meaning in words and giving those words back their value; to all those who wish to develop their capacity to listen, learn to appreciate proper dialogue, and take pleasure in talking with others. It will be a place for collective civic initiatives in the spirit of humanism.

We also address ourselves to all institutions which have as their vocation the cultivation and support of the arts of speech, whether their focus is on practical activity, performance, the creation of new works or their transmission, information, or education. We address all institutions which strive to help us enhance our ability to create meaning with words and promote a critical spirit toward all the manifold phenomena of speech. These are institutions which, by teaching the arts of speech and cultivating language, try to create social bonds and foster a culture of listening and of dialogue, in the interest of developing civic responsibility. They seek to create the conditions under which speech which has up to now been ignored can finally be heard.

We address ourselves to all civic associations, local administrations, and community groups who see themselves as working to make the way in which citizens speak to each other in the public realm more responsible, who are committed to promoting dialogue and listening with respect to what others have to say. All those associations, that is, which try to promote a sense of responsibility, civic engagement, and the critical spirit, and allow differences to express themselves, while at the same time defusing potentially violent confrontations, and which seek to restore debate to its proper place and give it back its proper value, to educate people in the use of the instruments of speech and mobilize the arts in the service of our common interest, an interest in creating human relations that are truly humane.

We address ourselves to all enterprises which can be benefited by improved speech: by the creation of meaning, of connection, and of openness; by encouraging people to listen to each other; by supporting dialogue; by fostering exchange and de-escalating potentially violent situations; by promoting respect; by creating bonds between members of the team and building team spirit; by giving priority to the human dimension; by a revitalization of immediate human presence; by laying the foundations for commitment; by learning to conceive, to express oneself, to transmit and share speech, to learn and relearn how to speak to each other.

We address ourselves to all associations devoted to the promotion of proper speech as the foundation of our humanity. In order to give people hope for the future; to open a perspective; to restore our dignity; to shape and reshape ourselves progressively; to improve and raise ourselves to a higher level; to go beyond ourselves and explore language; to get access to meaning and establish a relation with ourselves, others, and the world; to understand, experiment with, practise, and learn the arts of speech; to take pleasure in speaking to each other.

### A conversation with many voices

Who are we? I said at the start that we are artists of speech in the widest sense of the term. We are creators, performers, interpreters, artisans, spokespeople, keepers of the flame and relay racers who pass it on, authors, practitioners, literary types, theatre folk, musicians, people in the media, people devoted to art, to erudition and cognition, to local knowledge, to dialogue. We spend our lives on stage, in front of backdrops, behind lecterns, on platforms, around tables, in orchestra pits, in front of microphones, with scripts in our hands. We live by the word and we propagate the word. We are men and women who in the very heart of our creative activities, of what we do and produce and bring to life and set in motion, always struggle to be worthy vehicles of speech in the full sense.

We are artists, philosophers, novelists, orators, dramatists, essayists, producers, slammers, musicians, actors, poets, composers, reporters, lecturers, narrators, humourists, singers, editors, directors. All of us, taken together, collectively instantiate the seven arts of speech; we are vehicles of speech in the strong sense.

### Bringing together all people of good will

Although our project has its roots in a singular vision, its sense can only be collective. This is why the 'I' of the text now modulates into a 'we'. As a merely individual, isolated fragment of speech, this manifesto would be worthless. It would be even more worthless if speech became the private property of some particular group. It has to be open to all in order to have value. Only then can speech realize its full humanistic potential. Only by unleashing its full power can we make speech live again and give it back its value as an integral part of personal dignity and as a common good. This requires us to raise it to the level of an art and learn to deploy it correctly. In doing so, we realize our humanity in a more elevated form.

This is why, in the context of our attempt to give an artistic solution to a civic problem and as part of our mission to improve the moral and political health of the public sphere in our society, we envisage trying to establish cooperative relations with the largest possible number of people and organizations. Our goal is to mobilize the widest range of collective powers and individual energies possible in order to initiate a large-scale movement.

The direction in which we wish to move is toward assembling around our programme and our actions all those people of good will who wish to struggle against the degradation of speech. We wish to put an end to the use of speech as a pure means of domination; to brutal, senseless ersatz eloquence which is obsessed with obtaining immediate tangible results;

to speech as a tool which enables us to act on others as if they did not really exist. We wish to break with the culture of just broadcasting one's own views and never listening, of presumptuously taking liberties with others and humiliating them. We want to reverse the process in which people stop paying attention to each other and to the consequent progressive degradation of human relations so that individuals are thrown back utterly on themselves in a solitude that is only enhanced by existing in a world dominated by 'social' media. We say 'no' to the systemic aggression of this world, to the methodical bullying which is an inherent part of it, to the stultifying schematization of thought, feeling, and attitude which it fosters. We reject a world of blind stigmatization, radical intolerance, and repression of the Other, where everyone retreats behind a screen, language dies off, human links atrophy, and society is torn apart. Where speech is mutilated and humanity truncated.

We want to bring together all those who want to push themselves out of their comfort zone and make peace with others, who wish to speak to others and establish links with them, instead of engaging in mutual slaughter. We need to go beyond the idea of speaking 'well' – of eloquent speech – to the ideal of 'right speech'. We wish to elevate the whole domain of speech in order to transcend violence, to improve our own condition through cultivating these collective, constructive arts, the seven arts of speech, and to expand our possibilities through the creative and communicative activities and the forms of interaction which they permit and enhance. Speech, as we envisage it, is to be the incarnation of meaning, of connectedness with other people, of skill, and of responsibility. Fully vital speech is an art of listening, of living, of being fully present, of openness to the Other, and of cooperation. This is what we all aspire to as people who wish to realize all the promises that our humanity holds out to us, and who wish thereby to be humans capable of keeping our word.

What we strive for, in the end, is a peaceful society of accomplished individuals who express the quintessence of humanity and are impelled to realize the best possible versions of themselves. Who proclaim themselves people of their word. To be able to attain this also constitutes an art, one of the supreme arts, one of those which give meaning to life.

So through the cultivation and practice of speech in this sense can one hope that something will be regained? And if so, what? Not Paradise perhaps, but Humanity.

It depends only on us to start working in that direction.

# Notes

## Foreword

1 Simone de Beauvoir, 'Must We Burn Sade?', trans. Annette Michelson, in *The Marquis de Sade: 120 Days of Sodom and Other Writings*, trans. Austryn Wainhouse and Richard Seaver (Grove Weidenfeld, 1966), pp. 3–64.

2 Thucydides, *History of the Peloponnesian War*, Book 2, Chapter 65.

3 Ludwig Wittgenstein, *Tractatus Logico-Philosophicus*, trans. D.F. Pears and B.F. McGuinness (Routledge, 1961), 6.43.

## Chapter 1  Watch how you speak

1 Molière, *L'École des femmes* (Act I, Scene 1; vv. 161–4): '*L'autre jour (pourrait-on se le persuader?)/ elle était fort en peine, et vint me demander,/ avec une innocence à nulle autre pareille,/ si les enfants qu'on faut se faisaient par l'oreille* [The other day (if you can believe it),/ she was distraught and came to ask me,/ in all innocence, whether it was true that babies were made through the ears].'

2 Thucydides, *History of the Peloponnesian War*, Book II, Chapter 22. The Greek expression is κτῆμα ἐς ἀιεί.

3 Ray Bradbury, *Fahrenheit 451*, in *Novels & Story Cycles*, ed.

Jonathan R. Eller (The Library of America, 2021), p. 264: 'Where's your common sense? None of those books agree with each other. You've been locked up here for years with a regular damned Tower of Babel. Snap out of it! The people in those books never lived.'

4  Sophocles, *Philoctetes*, vv. 97–9.

5  Homer, *Odyssey*, Book I, vv. 1–2.

6  Aristoteles, *On the Generation of Animals*, Book II, Chapter 5, 741b.

7  Diogenes Laertius, *Lives of Eminent Philosophers*, Book VI, Chapter 40.

8  Plato, *Theaetetus*, 189d. Literally the passage reads: 'What do you call "thinking"'? The discourse which the soul conducts with itself about those things which it is considering.'

9  Antonin Artaud, 'To Have Done with the Judgment of God, a Radio Play (1947)', in Antonin Artaud, *Selected Writings*, ed. Susan Sontag (University of California Press, 1988), p. 571.

## Chapter 2  The Other does not exist

1  Lana and Lilly Wachowski (dirs), *The Matrix* (Warner Bros, 1999), sequence starting at 1:37:50.

2  Sigmund Freud, *A General Introduction to Psychoanalysis*, trans. G. Stanley Hall (Horace Liveright, 1920), p. 3.

3  Georg Wilhelm Friedrich Hegel, *Introduction to the Philosophy of History*, trans. John Sibree (Colonial Press, 1899), p. 18.

4  Fyodor Dostoevsky, *The Possessed*, trans. Constance Garnett (Macmillan, 1913), p. 374.

5  Friedrich Nietzsche, *The Gay Science*, trans. Walter Kaufmann (Vintage, 1974), §§273–5.

6  Molière, *Tartuffe*, Act III, Scene 5, vv. 1077–8.

7  Francis Ford Coppola (dir.), *The Godfather* (Paramount, 1972).

8  Margaret Atwood, *The Handmaid's Tale* (Vintage, 2016), p. 193.

9  William Shakespeare, *Othello*, Act IV, Scene 2.

10  Fritz Lang (dir.), *M* (*M – Eine Stadt sucht einen Mörder*) (Nero-Filmgesellschaft, 1931), sequence starting at 1:38:43.

11  George Orwell, *1984* (Penguin, 1954), p. 215.

12  Suzanne Collins, *The Hunger Games* (Scholastic, 2009), p. 22.

13  Sergio Leone (dir.), *The Good, the Bad and the Ugly* (*Il buono, il brutto, il cattivo*) (Produzioni Europee Associati, 1966), sequence starting at 2:49:15.

14  Milan Kundera, *The Art of the Novel*, trans. Linda Asher (Grove Press, 1986), p. 18.

## Chapter 3  Subject not at home

1  Talmud, *Shabbath* 31a: 'What is hateful to you, do not do it to your neighbour. This is the whole of the Law, everything else is commentary.'

2  Leviticus 19:18; Luke 6:31.

3  Immanuel Kant, *Groundwork of the Metaphysics of Morals*, trans. Mary Gregor (Cambridge University Press, 1997).

4  Arthur Rimbaud, 'Délires I': 'Vierge folle', in *Une saison en enfer* (Gallimard, 1984), p. 135.

5  Albert Camus, 'Noces à Tipasa', in *Noces suivi de l'Été* (Gallimard, 1959), pp. 18–19.

6  Augustine, *Confessions*, Book XI, chapter 20.

7  As in the 1967 song 'Le Téléfon' by Nino Ferrer: '*Gaston y a l'téléfon qui son/ et y a jamais person [sic] qui répond* [Gaston, the phone is ringing,/ but no one ever answers.'

8  Antoine de Saint-Exupéry, *The Little Prince*, trans. Katherine Woods (Egmont, 2001), p. 46.

9  Edgar Allen Poe, 'The Man of the Crowd', in *Poetry, Tales, and Selected Essays* (The Library of America, 1996), p. 396.

10  Charles Baudelaire, 'Les foules', in *Le Spleen de Paris* (Robert Laffont, 1980), p. 170.

11  For instance: https://www.healthcentral.com/condition/anxiety/glossophobia-fear-of-public-speaking. See also, for example, David L. Rowland and Jacques J.D.M Van Lankveld, 'Anxiety and Performance in Sex, Sport and Stage: Identifying Common Ground', *Frontiers of Psychology*, vol. 10 (July 2019), art. 1615, p. 9.

## Chapter 4  Standing by our words

1  Molière, *Le Misanthrope*, Act I, Scene 1, vv. 35–6.
2  In an apocryphal text which appeared under the title *La confession de Talleyrand* (Sauvaitre, 1891), p. 18.
3  Molière, *Le mariage forcé*, Scene 4.
4  Shakespeare, *Othello*, Act I, Scene 1.
5  Racine, *Britannicus*, Act II, Scene 3, vv. 681–2.
6  Ludwig Wittgenstein, *Tractatus Logico-Philosophicus*, trans. D.F. Pears and B.F. McGuinness (Routledge, 1961), 7.
7  Nicolas Boileau, *Art poétique* (Flammarion, 1998), p. 91.
8  Victor Hugo, 'Utilité du beau', in *Proses philosophiques des années 1860–1865* (*Œuvres complètes*) (Robert Laffont, 1985), pp. 581–5.
9  Latin *in* (privative) + *fari* (speak), so the infant is a human who is not yet able to speak.
10  Ferdinand de Saussure, *Course in General Linguistics*, trans. Wade Baskin (Philosophical Library, 1959), Chapters 3–4.
11  The word for the Christian Gospel, the 'good news', in Greek is *euangellion*: that is, *eu* ('good') and *angello* ('announce').
12  Michel Serres, *Thumbelina: The Culture and Technology of Millennials*, trans. Daniel W. Smith (Rowman & Littlefield, 2015).

## Chapter 5  Elevating speech

1  Albert Camus, *The First Man*, trans. David Hapgood (Alfred A. Knopf, 1995), p. 65.
2  Shakespeare, *Richard III*, Act I, Scene 1.
3  LEGO website: 'The LEGO Group History': https://www.lego.com/en-gb/aboutus/lego-group/the-lego-group-history?locale=en-gb.

## Chapter 6  The seven arts of speech.
## Cultivating our humanity

1  Philippe Jaccottet, 'Le travail du poète' (from *L'ignorant*), in *Poésie 1946–1967* (Gallimard, 1994), p. 64.
2  The question of whether Shakespeare is as valuable as a pair of

shoes is one that runs through much of Russian literature, from Tolstoy to Dostoevsky: 'The whole difficulty lies in the question which is more beautiful, Shakespeare or boots, Raphael or petroleum?', in Fyodor Dostoevsky, *The Possessed*, trans. Constance Garnett (Macmillan, 1913), p. 454. In his theatrical adaptation of Dostoevsky's novel, Camus sums up the debate: 'LIPOUTINE: We must think of the most urgent first. The most urgent need is for everyone to be able to eat. Books, art galleries, theaters are for later on, later on. . . . A pair of shoes is worth more than Shakespeare. STEPAN: Oh, I can't admit this. No, no, my good friend, immortal genius shines over all mankind. Let everyone go barefoot and long live Shakespeare. . . .' In Albert Camus, *The Possessed: A Play in Three Parts*, trans. Justin O'Brien (Alfred A. Knopf, 1960), p. 15.

3  Louis Aragon, *La Diane française* (Seghers, 2021), pp. 19–20.

4  F.W.J. Schelling, *The Philosophy of Art*, trans. Douglas W. Stott (University of Minnesota Press, 2008).

5  'Poetry' here is a synonym for 'literature'. Victor Hugo, 'Préface de Cromwell', in *Théâtre I* (Pléiade, 1963), pp. 422–3.

6  Marc Fumaroli, *L'âge de l'éloquence. Rhétorique et 'res literaria' de la Renaissance au seuil de l'époque classique* (Albin Michel, 1994).

7  Paul Verlaine, *La bonne chanson. Jadis et Naguère. Parallèlement* (Gallimard, 1979), p. 56.

8  Antoine Vitez, *Le théâtre des idées* (Gallimard, 1994), pp. 199–220.

9  Pierre Corneille, *Le Cid*, Act I, Scene 6.

10  From the Greek word *poiein*, 'to make, construct, compose, produce'.

11  André Gide, *The Counterfeiters*, trans. Dorothy Bussy (Alfred A. Knopf, 1927), p. 327.

12  *Republic*, 544c–546b.

### Chapter 7  The Centre for the Arts of Speech

1  Jean Vilar, 'Le TNP, service public', in *Le Théâtre, service public* (Gallimard, 1975), p. 173.

2 Antoine Vitez, 'Note sure le théâtre populaire', in *Écrits sur le théâtre* (P.O.L., 1998), p. 64; cf. p. 178.

3 Victor Hugo, *William Shakespeare*, Book V, 'Les esprits et les masses', in *Œuvres complètes* (Albin Michel, 1937), p. 168.

4 Régis Debray, *Cours de médiologie générale* (Gallimard, 1991), pp. 387–91.